Fight The Good Fight:

Getting Up After Life Knocks You Down

By Kerry Pharr

Foreword By

Zig Ziglar

Copyright © 2007 by Kerry Pharr

Fight The Good Fight:
Getting Up After Life Knocks You Down
by Kerry Pharr

Printed in the United States of America

ISBN 978-1-60266-480-7

All rights reserved solely by the author. The author guarantees all contents are original and do not infringe upon the legal rights of any other person or work. No part of this book may be reproduced in any form without the permission of the author. The views expressed in this book are not necessarily those of the publisher.

Unless otherwise indicated, Bible quotations are taken from New King James Version or paraphrased by the author. Copyright © 1988 by Thomas Nelson, Inc.

www.xulonpress.com

Dedication

Herbert Hoover Pharr, my Dad, died while we were finishing this book. I spoke to him and prayed with him the morning of his death. He entered the hospital for what we all thought was a minor medical procedure.

"I'll call you this afternoon and let you know how everything turned out," he said.

He was confident that he was going to live much longer. The procedure seemingly went fine. However, a couple of hours later he went into cardiac arrest and died.

A story about my life would be incomplete without sharing a little about him and my family. As a young man my dad lived a wild life apart from God. He loved to drink, party and gamble. Mother didn't drive and dad didn't go to church. I remember the trying times when he would not return home for several days. Those early days were very difficult on our dear Christian mother, who was left alone much of the time to raise six children —Louie, Jerry, Patricia, Martha, Janet and me (Kerry).

I was the oldest child, but I did not provide a positive example for my younger siblings. Instead, I was a wild, rebellious son who inflicted much sadness and pain to my mother's life. Mother, please forgive me for being wicked in my youth.

This is a story about personal redemption. It's a story about a family that was lost and dying without hope. Then, a merciful God sent a couple of dear saints, to our home who offered to take our family to church. As a result, all of our family – even Dad – came to discover the wonders of Jesus Christ. We discovered that His power would carry us through both triumphs and travails.

But, before finding the Lord, my father strayed and lived the life of a sinner. After I had married and moved away, my 42-year-old father still was partying in the local bars. One night he got into a fight with someone and afterward, in a moment of clarity, he reflected about his wayward living. He came home drunk, went to bed and fell asleep. He woke up a short time later, feeling burdened about the way he lived life. He got down on his knees and began to pray. In the middle of the night, he asked my mother to wake up my five siblings to pray for him.

He cried out to the Lord for help, repented of his sins, and gave his life to Christ. He turned away from his old lifestyle. Immediately, he quit his lifelong habits of smoking cigarettes and drinking alcohol. He started attending church regularly, becoming a devoted family man. God changed his heart completely, and for the next 35 years he lived for Christ. He didn't return to the bars, except to tell his friends what Christ had done in his life. As I write this, Mother is still alive, but is in the final stages of Alzheimer's disease.

I dedicate this book to my parents, Herbert and Jessie Pharr. Because of Christ, we'll spend eternity together in a perfect new world free of sickness, pain or suffering. There will be no sadness; there and no goodbyes. What a blessed hope we have in Jesus.

Acknowledgements

Thanks to Zig Ziglar, my Sunday school teacher in Dallas and a nationally recognized author and motivational speaker and teacher, who encouraged me to finish the book when I had written only one story. Without his encouragement, I would not have had the confidence to continue the writing process. Thanks for being "Mr. Encouragement."

Thanks to my good friend David Hudson, a Nashville-based attorney, author, boxing judge and all-around good guy for his final edits, suggestions and help in getting the manuscript ready for publishing.

Thanks to Randy Weiler, my good friend for nearly 30 years. He was a *Nashville Banner* sportswriter for 21-plus years and reported many of our boxing team's successes and failures. Randy also helped by reviewing and editing much of the early manuscript. He also lent his keen eye to copy-editing. Thanks to Tanya Davis for her help in reorganizing and editing the manuscript. Thanks to David Gunzel for your suggestions and recommendations.

Thanks to my extended and immediate family – cousins Phillip Pharr and Brenda Warren, Phillip's wife, Debbie, my uncle, Grady Pharr and my Dad, Herbert, for helping me recall details of some events reported in the book.

Fight The Good Fight

Thanks to my sister, Patricia Petree, for her research at the Kenosha, Wisconsin, Library.

I also deeply appreciated and benefited from the encouragement of my wife, Lanita, and my daughter, Christy Campbell. They were behind me totally as I worked on this project.

I'm grateful to have known and been associated with everyone mentioned in the book, and I want to thank you for allowing me to share part of your life.

Most of all I am grateful to my Lord, Jesus Christ, for saving my soul and allowing me to tell my story so that others may come to know Him, also.

Table of Contents

Fight the Good Fight

Dedication v

Acknowledgements vii

Table of Contents ix

    Chapter 1:   Human Strength and Life's Pressures 13

    Chapter 2:   Early Years 23

    Chapter 3:   My Boxers 65

    Chapter 4:   Women of Steel 95

    Chapter 5:   Life Lessons 69

    Chapter 6:   Advice for New Christians 129

    Chapter 7:   Heavyweight Champions and Would Be Contenders 153

    Chapter 8:   Battling Depression and Addictions 229

Foreword

Kerry Pharr writes an interesting book. The memories he shares of his career in the boxing world are at times exciting, while at other times they are tinged with sadness. Readers familiar with boxing will find his reminiscences fascinating; those not caught up in the fight world will learn much about the business as well as the personalities of that genre.

The heart of Kerry's story is his faith in and relationship with Christ, and how that dynamic influenced and affected the choices and decisions he made throughout the years. He very capably establishes a comparison of his life, as well as the lives of the fighters, with and without the love and forgiveness of our Lord.

If you enjoy history, personal anecdotes and human-interest stories, I believe you will enjoy *Fight the Good Fight*.

Zig Ziglar
Author/Motivational Speaker/Teacher

Chapter 1: Human Strength and Life's Pressures

Reconciling Christianity and Boxing

How can a born-again Christian be involved in a sport commonly perceived to be brutal, corrupt and immoral? There is a reason that boxing has been called "the red light district of sports." It is filled with deceitful people.

As a Christian who truly desired to live by the teachings of Jesus Christ, I wrestled with these questions of morality many times during my more than 20-year involvement with professional boxing.

The public perceives professional boxing as a barbaric, brutal and crooked sport. Critics claim this vicious sport should be outlawed. Although boxing has its share of flaws, there is a more positive side to the sport that captures the heart and mind of young men (and now women) who aspire to become champions.

Boxing's image hasn't always been so tarnished and trashed. Former President Theodore Roosevelt praised the sport for its instillation of discipline and hearty exercise. In the 1920s and '30s, boxing was called the manly art of self-defense. It remains a real art and a manly sport where men (and women) exhibit great courage, endurance and perseverance. In Teddy's day, boxing was considered an admirable and honorable endeavor second in popularity only to professional baseball.

The first amateur boxing championships in the United States took place in 1923 when the *Chicago Tribune* sponsored a citywide amateur boxing tournament. The winner received a golden glove pin and the tournament fittingly was named the Golden Gloves. Newspapers across America began to sponsor Golden Gloves boxing tournaments and soon a national Golden Gloves tournament was held each year in either Chicago or New York. This continued until the early 1970s as newspapers sponsored tournaments across the country. These amateur tournaments were great sporting events. Local Golden Gloves champions were admired, respected and treated like celebrities. Such was the climate when I was introduced to the sport at age 11. It wasn't until I was an adult and intimately involved that I learned about the seedy side to professional boxing.

Boxing is a craft that takes many years to master. Learning the art develops speed, courage, endurance and self-confidence. If I had a son or grandson who wanted to learn self-defense, I would teach him how to box as an amateur.

The author's daughter, Christy Campbell, and granddaughter, Cambryn, 7, carry on a family tradition by studying Karate.

In amateur boxing the safety of the athlete is the No. 1 priority of everyone involved. The boxers wear protective headgear, a mouthpiece and a protective cup to protect the area below the belt. Amateur boxers' hands are wrapped with gauze and tape. They also wear large gloves to lessen the power of the punches. As long as the athletes are competitively matched and the officials protect the participants, I believe amateur boxing is still a great sport that is no more dangerous than high school football.

The problems with professional boxing are a different matter. Money is involved. All of the deadly sins associated with money – greed, corruption, lying, cheating, disloyalty and stealing – run rampant throughout the sport.

These problems in boxing presented me with challenging questions during my tenure in professional boxing. In the following pages, I will share some of those stories with you, along with the mistakes and personal failures this Christian has made in my life and career in professional boxing.

You will read about the lessons I learned and how I attempted to serve the Lord while participating in the boxing world as a manager, trainer and promoter for more than 20 years.

Ironically, I found that boxing and my Christian faith worked hand-in-hand, like a great combination of punches. My Christian faith served as the foundation that allowed me to survive and even thrive in the unseemly world of professional boxing. The sport also enabled me to help many young men who needed an outlet from negative influences in their lives.

'They're Shooting Blanks.
Let's Get Them!'

Jay and Woody, two acquaintances from my rebellious youth, were about to walk into Doug's Bar, a tavern located on 63rd Street in Kenosha, Wisconsin, one warm July evening. I knew these individuals well, as a 19-year-old who used a fake identification card to gain entry into the bars. Jay and Woody were in their early 30s and I'd see them around town occasionally.

Jay was a compact, muscular guy with a vise-like grip. He wasn't mean, but he was known in the local bars as a person not to mess with. He had a reputation as someone who would hurt others if provoked. He had already whipped one of my tough cousins in a street fight.

As they were about to enter the bar, Jay and Woody heard a disturbance from across the street. Looking up, they saw two teenagers attacking an elderly man – rolling him for his money.

"Let's help that old man!" Woody said.

The two grown men raced across the street and grabbed the teenagers, slinging them around like rag dolls. Almost immediately, they heard a loud burst of gunfire as one of the teenagers pointed a pistol at them and began firing.

Woody shouted, "Jay, they're shooting blanks. Let's get them!"

Suddenly, Jay fell to the sidewalk, dead before he hit the ground. In the chaos and excitement Woody had also been hit in the arm, but didn't even realize it. Woody survived, but Jay – without any warning or an opportunity to prepare for it – lost his life in an instant. His physical strength and prowess was unable to deliver him from the armed youngster.

Jay went into eternity to meet the Lord. The teen that shot Jay and Woody was only 14.

Fight The Good Fight

Life is so fragile and sometimes very violent. Things can change beyond our control in an instant.

I once worked for a relatively young man who was wealthy enough to own an airplane. He traveled in that plane regularly. One morning after visiting his daughter, who was in college in another state, he boarded the plane he was piloting. Immediately after takeoff, something went terribly wrong with one of the engines and the plane crashed. He perished instantly.

I'm certain that the people in the World Trade Center felt very comfortable and secure in those buildings on the morning of Sept. 11, 2001. However, many of them would violently lose their lives before the day ended because of murderous Islamic radicals who killed them in the name of their god, Allah.

The news media recently has run rampant with the story of Anna Nicole Smith's sudden and unexplained death. Her story is of one who became famous by doing infamous things. She had been a stripper, a *Playboy* centerfold and a model. She married a billionaire 60 years her senior, and then battled his children and heirs in court over the estate after he died. In 2006, she gave birth to a daughter. Her 20-year-old son was found dead in her recovery room, evidently of a drug overdose. Now, her young daughter is without a mother. What a sad, tragic, empty life filled with heartache and pain. Reportedly, she had battled drug addiction.

In an unexpected moment, her life on earth ended. We are all going to face death. According to Hebrews 9:27 ("And as it is appointed for men to die once, but after this the judgment."), we actually have an appointment with death and after that judgment for the things we do here on earth. Being rich, famous, or powerful doesn't insulate anyone from facing God and giving an account of their life here on earth.

Who Am I, and Why Should You Read My Story?

I'm Kerry Pharr and I have devoted 40 years of my life to the sport of boxing, the so-called "Sweet Science." I've been an amateur boxer, coach, trainer, corner man, promoter and writer. I've also served as a member of the Tennessee Boxing Advisory Board, which makes recommendations to state officials on rules and regulations. I've spent time with the big names, the lesser-known and countless fans. More importantly, I'm a Christian – a rarity in a decidedly secular sport seeped in sin.

It wasn't always that way. As a youngster, I was a juvenile delinquent – a rugged background for a Christian man, wouldn't you say? But, that's the beauty of Christianity – even the worst of sinners can find redemption. The great Moses killed a man early in his life.

I'm here today to share my story with you – not only the entertaining, exciting parts of the sport, but also the darker parts. I'll share boxing stories as well as life truths. You don't need to be a boxer or even an athlete to relate to these stories.

Before I share with you some personal encounters with pro boxing legends Muhammad Ali, George Foreman, Thomas Hearns, the late Big John Tate and others later in the book, I want to reveal the long and winding road that led me down the boxing path.

I believe I was led to share my story, so that other people can find hope. Life can be a vicious struggle, but it doesn't have to be. As a Christian, I can promise you that there is hope in Jesus Christ. I hope you will enjoy this book, and pray that it might lead you closer to God and to your own personal redemption.

Dealing With the Pressures of Life

Joel Osteen of Houston, Texas, one of America's most popular preachers, tells of his mother being diagnosed with terminal metastases liver cancer more than 20 years ago. The doctors only gave her a few weeks to live and sent her home to die. Osteen tells how his mother never gave up. She refused to speak words of sickness or of death, but rather she began to quote scriptures of life. She recited verses like Psalm 118:17: "*I shall not die, but live and declare the works of the Lord.*"

She also found comfort and strength in Psalm 91:16: "*With long life I will satisfy him, and show him my salvation.*"

She placed photographs of her former, healthy self all around her house. She began feeding her mind and body messages of life and health. Soon she began to feel better, and eventually she was totally healed of the cancer. Mrs. Osteen had faith in God and faith in His promises. She constantly proclaimed them day and night, until they took root in her body and in her soul.

I don't believe there is anything more frightening than receiving a report from a doctor that you or one of your family members is terminally ill. It is like a blow to the stomach. It crushes a person's spirit and sometimes their will to live.

If you think you are defeated, you probably will be. But if you think you can overcome trials and tribulations, then don't run and hide. Instead, face these trials head on. Speak words of life instead of death. Don't lie down and quit. Fight, fight, fight!

The naysayer may tell you that you can't get well, or that you are going to lose your house, or go bankrupt. Don't believe those who tell you, that *you are going to lose your battle.* Sometimes your adversary isn't as powerful as you think it is, and many times when faced with difficult circum-

Fight The Good Fight

stances you are stronger than you realize. As long as you can breathe, you can fight to improve your circumstances.

There is an omnipotent and omniscient God in heaven that hears our prayers and longs to help us in our day-to-day lives. Go to God in prayer in the name of Jesus, and make your requests known to Him.

Read Philippians 4:6: *"Be anxious for nothing, but in every thing by prayer and supplication, with thanksgiving, let your requests be made known to God."*

Chapter 2: My Early Years

Life in Detroit

Mom and Dad had trouble in their marriage almost from the very beginning. My mother wanted a home and a family, but Dad wanted to drink, gamble and run around with his buddies. There were nights when he didn't come home at all. Many times on payday he would play poker and lose his entire paycheck.

This hurt and angered my mother. It created tension between my parents, and probably served to fuel the rage burning inside me.

After living in Birmingham, Alabama, for five years, Dad and several of his buddies traveled to Detroit, Michigan. They heard they could earn big money in the auto factories. He soon got a job at General Motors and moved our family there.

Detroit was much different from the South, and there was culture shock moving to an area where people thought that we were no-good, shiftless rednecks.

We lived in a three-room, second-story apartment in a building behind a mom-and-pop grocery store in a multiracial neighborhood across the street from the housing projects on 4th Street. We were just a few blocks from the old Tiger Stadium in downtown Detroit.

My father was gone most of the time, and my mother was sick and stayed in bed a lot during my formative years. So I would sneak off with a couple of other youngsters and roam the streets. I can remember walking down the street with another youngster when I was only 7 or 8, and having a couple of older kids shake us down for money. It was a rough neighborhood with muggers, drunks and sexual predators. One of my earliest memories is of the police arresting a drunk, naked woman walking down our street. They placed a blanket around her and took her away in a squad car.

One summer night, my mother gave me a small sum of money and sent me to the store. At the bottom of the steps, I turned and walked through a dark passageway between two buildings. When I stepped into the dark alley, a man grabbed me and tried to take my mother's money from me. I began hollering and my mother heard my cries from an open second-story window. She ran to that window and started screaming at the mugger. There were people on the street in front of our building, so the man let me go and ran off while I clutched the money tightly.

Another time, we couldn't find my sister Patricia, who had disappeared. I still can see Mother sitting in a police car crying hysterically. Several hours later, a teenager appeared with her by his side. He had taken her into an apartment building. She was only 4, and couldn't tell the police what had happened. We never knew if he had molested her.

To this day, Patricia has no recollection of that event. While living on 4th Street, my sister Martha was born. Years later, I returned to Detroit and looked for the old neighborhood, but it was gone. It had been burned down during the 1960s race riots.

Overcoming Hatred and Sexual Abuse

I've often said that it takes someone with a unique personality to be involved with boxing. How many people enjoy having someone punch his or her lights out every day? And how many people really enjoy beating someone else up? Many actually do. Is that normal? I don't know the answer to either of these questions, but in my case I experienced a lot of pain as a child that made me want to fight. Boxing gave me a sense of self-worth. Or perhaps the violent sport simply filled a void in my life. Many times I think of my childhood and try to determine what aroused such passion in my life for this brutal sport.

I can remember a gang of boys chasing me home from school many times when I was in elementary school. I often went out of my way so I wouldn't be attacked by a group of older kids. This was a time of great racial tension in America. Since I was from Alabama and many black people were being abused down South, it was assumed that I was a racist. I remember having a black schoolmate who was my friend. We'd go to each other's house looking in the refrigerator for something to eat, unconcerned about our differences.

I also was prey for a very dangerous person. This was an older man – a wolf in sheep's clothing who was a sexual deviate. Specifically, he liked little boys. When he got me alone, he sexually abused me. I hated him for what he did to me. I was traumatized and sickened by the repugnant act for many years. I'm ashamed to mention it even today, although I was a helpless child and victim. Even at such an early age, I knew there was something unnatural about that act. It repulsed me.

We soon moved to another area of Detroit and I don't know whatever happened to this man.

Fight The Good Fight

As a result of the way I had been sexually abused as a child, when I became a parent, I watched everyone around my daughter.

While I was still in Detroit as a youngster, a group of older boys decided to steal from a local grocery store. They took me with them and when we got to the store they put a carton of ice cream in a bag and ordered me to walk outside with it. Since I was young, I became very frightened and told them no. As they kept trying to make me carry it out of the store, I kept saying no until a store manager walked up and asked what we were doing. He determined that we were trying to steal something and he loaded all of us in a car, took us home and told our parents. Wouldn't you know it – Dad was at home this time. When the store manager told him what I had done, Dad immediately took off his belt and wore me out. My pleas of innocence went unheeded. There was no innocent until proven guilty. I was presumed guilty.

Everywhere I went during the next few weeks, I had to watch my back. The boys in the neighborhood blamed me for getting caught at the store, and they were after me.

There were those who thought they were a higher class of people and they put us down, calling us rednecks and hillbillies.

I remember one adult saying to me, "Why don't you hillbillies go back where you came from?"

The older boys constantly picked me on. The black kids in the neighborhood also ganged up on me, chasing me home from school because I was a white kid from Alabama.

I became a very angry and bitter young man at age 8. I wanted to learn how to fight so I could stop all of these people from hurting me.

After I finished third grade, Dad was laid off from his General Motors job. We moved south to live with my grandparents. Happiness for me was seeing Detroit in the rearview mirror of my dad's old Hudson car.

Fight The Good Fight

The next 18 months or so that we lived in the South was a wonderful time in my life. My parents desperately tried to find jobs while they were there, but aside from farming, there was virtually no industry in the rural South. Dad had a couple of relatives who were working at American Motors, an auto factory in Kenosha, Wisconsin. After several months of job hunting in the South without success, my father and mother went north. My father got a job at American Motors while my mother landed a job at a candy factory. Since they were trying to get on their feet financially, they left my two sisters with Dad's parents, who were retired.

Four Rooms and a Path

My mind often drifts to cherished memories of a dusty gravel road in the countryside where I once lived. My parents were born in rural Mississippi and Alabama. Mother was born in a little town called Tremont, Mississippi, 30 miles east of Tupelo, the birthplace of Elvis Presley. Country singing legend Tammy Wynette also was from Tremont and was best friends with my cousin, Linda Loden. My uncle, Glen Hargett, had dated Tammy when they were teenagers. My father was born just across the state line in Vina, Alabama, where our Irish ancestors had settled in the 1830s.

Dad was a local high school football standout, starring as the Vina Red Devils' quarterback. Mother dropped out of school in the 10th grade and went to beauty college. After finishing beauty school, she opened a small hair salon in Vina. She and Dad met and married after he graduated from high school. They moved to Birmingham, Alabama. Dad interviewed for a job at the Hormel meat company.

The man who interviewed him for the job asked him, "Son, have you ever done any hard work?"

To which Dad replied, "That's all I've ever done my whole life."

He was hired, and he and Mom soon started a family. I was the firstborn. Later, my younger brother Louie and sister Patricia also were born in Birmingham.

My parents had grown up on the farm and decided they wanted a better life. Farming in the 1940s was extremely hard. The poor rural farmers didn't have tractors. They plowed their fields with a team of mules. In those days, Dad and his brothers would walk behind a team of mules with a plow in hand. Even as late as 1959, when I was old enough to help work on the farm, my grandfather still had a mule team and a wagon. I remember helping pull corn that fall by hand and throwing it onto the wagon.

Fight The Good Fight

The days I spent on the farm and traveled on those dusty gravel roads with my parents and grandparents are some of my sweetest memories. Life was tough, but those were the greatest of times when I felt loved as part of a family.

My younger brother Louie and I lived with my maternal grandparents, O.G. and Vera Hargett, for one year and also a couple of summers to help them on the farm. They lived in a four-room house that had a path instead of a bath. The path led to the outhouse that was situated about 150 yards behind the house.

We didn't have running water in the house the year we lived with Mom-Maw and Pop Paw. We carried our bathing and drinking water from a natural spring about 50 yards from the house. It was the purest, best-tasting water imaginable. In winter, we heated the house with a wood-burning stove and bathed in a metal dishpan. In summer, on Sunday mornings before church, Pop Paw would take Louie and me to a spring-fed pond on our Uncle Bob's property, where we would swim and get our weekly bath.

In the evening after eating we'd sit outside on an old porch swing and talk for hours. Relatives often came by to visit or for Sunday dinner. My grandmother fixed the best fried chicken in the world, and no one has ever come close to making a coconut pie as good as hers. . Although these days were hard as far as the way we lived, they were heaven to me in comparison to my time in Detroit.

My brother and I were given our own hoe and a new straw hat. We learned so much from my maternal grandparents while working by their side on the farm. Louie and I walked many miles beside them with a hoe in our hands as we chopped cotton day after day in that hot Mississippi sun. Pop Paw taught me a lot about working hard and giving more than I received. He would say, "I always like to give a man more of a day's work than he pays me for." He also said, "When you are working for someone else, it's OK to

Fight The Good Fight

stop working if the boss stops to talk to you, but don't stop and talk to anyone else." He taught me that a man's word is his bond and to be honorable in my business dealings. Mom Maw fed us like kings. She knew that my brother and I were finicky about what we ate, but we loved her cooking. Our favorite was her fried chicken. If one of my uncles killed a rabbit or a squirrel while hunting I'm certain it ended up on the dinner table. Whenever we would ask Mom-Maw what she was frying for supper, she would always reply chicken. Since she said it was chicken, we always ate it. The work was hard, but the family time we shared with them was oh, so sweet.

Standing Up to the Bully and Becoming One of the Boys

When I went to school in the fall in Mississippi and the local boys learned that I had lived up north, they would taunt me and say, "You're a Yankee."

"I am not! I was born in Alabama," I declared.

One day a group of about 10 boys stood in front of me. The leader, a kid who had failed three grades in school, said, "Since you're a Yankee, you've got to fight one of us. So you pick the one you want to fight."

I don't know why, but I told the older boy, "I'll fight you."

We began fighting. He was much bigger than me, so he bounced me around like a rubber ball. But I didn't quit, and when the fight was finished, I was accepted as one of the gang. They never called me a Yankee again. It was a great feeling to finally be accepted by someone.

During my pre-teen days in the rural South, I spent most of my spare time with my cousin, Jimmy Lucas. There wasn't a lot to do in the country like there was in the city, so we passed our time by playing baseball or swimming in the nearby creek. We also loved to explore the woods and its snake-infested swamp.

For fun, we would declare war on wasps and poisonous snakes. Those big red wasps were everywhere. You could walk innocently by a wasp nest and get stung before you saw the wasp coming toward you. Once we were stung, we would cry or scream out in agony for about a full minute. Then we would declare war on the wasps and go to the barn to find a giant wasp nest to destroy.

As a weapon against the wasps, we took a cane fishing pole and put a rag soaked in gasoline on the end of it. Once we found a wasp nest, we carefully placed the end of the cane pole with the gasoline-soaked rag on it on the wasp nest. This killed some of the wasps, but it infuriated the rest. Instantly, an army of wasps came after us. We dropped the fishing pole and ran for our lives, but these wasps attacked us like jet fighter pilots as they dive-bombed us with their stingers.

As much as a wasp sting hurts, it is much more painful to get stung by a hornet or a yellow jacket. Some of these insects have nests in trees or on buildings while others have nests in the ground. Wasp stings are similar to the hard realities we face in life. Circumstances hit us by surprise and hurt just like a painful sting. We feel the pain because it is real. When we don't focus on the pain it soon disappears. Rev. Robert Schuller once said, "Tough times don't last, but tough people do." If we carry on in our lives, the pain will disappear and become a distant memory

On a hot summer day, I was mowing the lawn at Uncle Bob and Aunt Exie Lucas' house. Exie is my mother's older sister. My cousins, Jimmy and Joan, were sitting inside the house. While mowing the front lawn, I felt something hit the blade of the lawnmower. I heard a very rapid sound of *ping, ping, ping, ping* hitting the blade. Almost simultaneously I felt a large number of yellow jackets inside my pant legs, stinging me with a vengeance. They were angry and attacked me furiously.

The pain was enormous and I began to holler. I tried to run away from the incredible pain. I was making so much noise that both of my cousins Jimmy and Joan came outside to see the commotion. I ran around the house while slapping myself on the leg everywhere that I felt a sting. Finally, I reached the barnyard and jumped into the cattle water trough, unashamedly pulling my pants off as fast as I could. My legs were covered with stings from the yellow jackets. By this time, Jimmy and Joan were standing close by laughing hysterically.

Fight The Good Fight

The intense pain of those multiple stings is now a distant memory. On that hot summer day, they hurt me so badly that I screamed and cried. But the pain eventually went away and I carried on with my life. Now that experience is nothing more than a humorous memory.

You may be going through a painful experience in your life that really hurts right now. Don't focus on the pain. It will go away. Carry on with your life and someday soon that experience will fade into a distant memory.

Snakes

There are a lot of rattlesnakes, copperheads and water moccasins in the rural southern United States. Because these poisonous snakes are dangerous, you learn early in life to kill them when they are close to the house. Like our wars with wasps, killing snakes became a favorite pastime for my cousin Jimmy and me. If we saw a snake while we were chopping cotton, we would kill it with a hoe. If we saw one while we were on the tractor or in the pickup truck, we would run over it. There were snakes in the creek, so when we went swimming we would run in, splashing the water to scare away the snakes.

Most everyone living in the rural South has encountered at least one poisonous snake. Most folks have a healthy respect for and a fear of snakes. It is very easy to tease and scare people about snakes.

One hot August morning, my Dad arrived at my grand-parents' house. He had driven from Wisconsin all night, and was very tired from the 12-hour trip. There was no air conditioning at my Grandparents' house, so Dad laid a quilt on the ground underneath a Catawba tree and proceeded to take a nap.

Being the good son, I took a cane fishing pole and slid it very slowly up one of his pant legs. Dad felt something crawling up his leg and thought that it was a snake. Suddenly, he awakened and his body went into convulsions as he attempted to rid his pants of the intruder. Abruptly, he opened his eyes and noticed that the culprit was actually me. "Boy, if you try that again, I'll wear you out," he snarled. Then he closed his eyes and went back to sleep.

There is a real serpent called Satan that we face in life. The Bible tells us that he is our adversary and that he walks about like a roaring lion seeking people to destroy. (1 Peter 5:8) We are also told that he can transform himself into an

Fight The Good Fight

angel of light. In the Garden of Eden when he approached Eve in the form of a serpent tempting her to sin, he was very cunning. She was seduced by his charm and yielded to temptation by tasting the forbidden fruit that God had told her and Adam not to eat. (Genesis 3:1-6) We are admonished to be vigilant or to be on the lookout for him. Satan might come in the form of an alluring man or woman in your life. He might even be an enticing sweet drink in a cocktail glass or an illicit drug that you are tempted to try. It might be fame, fortune or power that he clothes himself with to capture your soul. All of these can be the serpent's cunning way of entrapping you so that he might ultimately destroy your life and damn your soul. Beware of the things that he might use to trap you.

My First Encounter with Boxing

Kenosha was a rough-and-tough blue collar Wisconsin factory town on Lake Michigan, about halfway between Chicago and Milwaukee. We were southern migrants to this northern factory city of about 70,000 people, but living there was much better than Detroit. There were several thousand other southerners who also had journeyed to this auto factory promised land, looking for a better way of life than working on the farm.

Many southerners lived in the trailer park including a beautiful sandy headed, blue-eyed girl named Diane Smith who was a year older than me. Her family was from Corinth, Mississippi. At age 11, I fell in love with her. She was very sweet and her family lived in a nice-looking trailer. I was the dirty, scruffy little boy who lived in what I perceived as a shack in the same park.

My mother was a Christian who had been beaten down by years of hard life and the hell that my dad had put her through. She didn't drive, and my dad wouldn't take our family to church. Mother prayed that the Lord would provide a way for her five children to go to church to hear about Jesus Christ. Some time later, Stella Tuttle and Pop Sharnick, who were members of First Assembly of God Church, visited our home on bus visitation. They asked my mother if she would allow her children to ride the bus to church on Sundays. This was an answer to my mother's prayers, and she made my siblings and me get on that bus and go to church. .

I was so embarrassed by our home that I would get on and off of that bus anywhere other than in front of our trailer. If Dad were home at all on Sundays, he would sleep until the afternoon football games. My mother wanted to go to church, but didn't drive. Eventually, she swallowed her pride and rode that bus to church with all her children.

I joined the Boy Scouts at age 11. Traditionally, the Boy Scouts were given tickets to the annual Golden Gloves boxing tournament held at the Kenosha Elks Club. One Tuesday night, I went with the Boy Scouts to see my first boxing match.

My Dad said, "Son, when you go to the boxing matches tonight, I want you to watch a fighter by the name of Larry Broughman. He's from Mississippi, and I work with his older brother. He's supposed to be pretty good."

That night as I watched the boxing, I was mesmerized. The auditorium was packed to capacity, and the crowd cheered on the local fighters, and stomped their feet on the hardwood floor. The noise from the cheering crowd was deafening, the excitement was amazing and the atmosphere was magical. I watched and cheered for Broughman as he won his bout that evening. He went on to win the Golden Gloves championship in his weight division several weeks later. I got so excited watching him fight that I couldn't wait until I was old enough to go to the boxing gym. Broughman was a good local fighter who never boxed professionally. The last time I heard about him he still was in Kenosha.

That night, I began a 40-year love affair with the sport of boxing. From that day forward, I was a boxing junkie. I saw boxing as something that I could use to protect myself, and also as something to repair my shattered self-image. For 40 years I had an abnormal love/hate relationship with the sport of boxing.

Hard Lessons Learned Early

Playing sports made me feel good and helped my self-esteem. Even though I was small at 5-foot-7 and 165 pounds, I was a good high school middle linebacker. I was on the track team in junior high school and won the city championship in the 60-yard dash and also first place as a member of our 440-relay team. I also competed in the bicycle races on the Washington Bowl veladrome.

I was quick and very aggressive in football, and I loved to hit people. During our high school scrimmages, I played so hard that I sent two or three of my own teammates to the hospital with broken bones. Our coach didn't want our quarterback banged up, so he finally made a rule that during scrimmages I couldn't touch him. I was only allowed to put pressure on him

On one particular play I didn't hear the coach tell us that we were going to *walk* through a field goal attempt by our kicker, Bill Luie. When the ball was snapped, I rushed through the line like I was on fire. Since it was a play that we were supposed to walk through, no one tried to block me. When I got within five feet of Bill, he kicked the ball in a perfect line drive that hit me squarely between the legs and sent me crumbling in agony to the ground. I always learned life's lessons the hard way.

Two Black Eyes

Mother tried her best to raise me to live righteously. The words of Merle Haggard's song "Mama Tried" seemed to sum up my rebellious teenage years: *"In spite of all my Sunday learning, toward the bad I kept on turning, till Momma couldn't hold me anymore."*

As I grew older, I began to do wild and crazy things. I always was doing something stupid and getting into trouble at school. Everywhere I went, I got into a fight After I came home with my second or third black eye as a teenager, Dad said to me, "Boy, the next time you come home with a black eye, I'm going to black the other one for you."

Soon afterward, I got into a fight at Washington Bowl, a local park that had a bicycle veladrome racetrack in it. There were about 100 spectators from school who watched me fight a fellow by the name of Mike Schwer. He gave me two black eyes that day. I was always a softhearted kid, and up until that time I was Mr. Nice Guy while in a fight. I didn't believe in hitting anyone in the face, so I would wrestle against my opponents while they used their fists against me. When I went home with both eyes black, all Dad could do was shake his head.

My cousin Phillip and I always were into mischief. In our early teens, we wandered the streets, aimlessly looking for something to do. We hung around the harbor a lot and watched the boats come in and out of Lake Michigan. One day we were standing on a bridge at the harbor and when a large boat passed underneath, we threw a brick onto the deck of the boat. Fortunately, no one was hit.

Years later, a young boxer, who had trained at my boxing gym, killed a soldier who just had returned home from the Gulf War. He threw a huge rock off of an interstate bridge onto the veteran's car. I'm so thankful that my stupidity didn't result in the death of someone else. Sean has been in prison all of his adult life because of this malicious act. Not knowing what Sean had done, I unwittingly hired him to do some work for me a couple of days after this tragic incident. I remember Sean laughing and joking like he didn't have a care in the world that afternoon as he, another local boxer and I worked together. The next evening I turned on the television to watch the 10 p.m. news. I was in shock and utter disbelief when the news anchor announced that the police just had arrested a suspect in the death of the soldier and showed Sean's photo. I physically was sickened by what I had just seen and heard on television. Immediately, I remembered seeing him the day before and remembered the way he had acted. It all seemed surreal. In my mind, I couldn't comprehend how someone could kill someone else and seemingly show no remorse. I personally felt guilty because he had been under my tutelage for a few months and although I had tried to minister to him I was unable to help him. I haven't seen or talked to Sean since. Someone told me that they saw him at a parole hearing and that he flexed his muscles in a most muscular pose directed at the fallen soldier's family. How sad.

One thing that Phillip and I were required to do with our fathers was to help them run their fishing trout lines on the Fox River. My dad and W.B. fished for catfish so often that they could have been commercial fishermen. When weather permitted, they lived on that river.

We spent many cold, wet nights on the banks of the Fox River. One cold night late in the fall, the four of us were fishing on the river. We had built a fire and were gathering more fire wood. Uncle W.B. (we called him Dub-Bee) grabbed a large limb and handed it to Phillip, then he said to me, "Kerry, jump on that thing and let's break it so we can use it for the fire."

Fight The Good Fight

Phillip was standing on the edge of the bank next to that cold, dark river. We just had caught a large, mean-looking snapping turtle about five minutes earlier.

I didn't know that the limb Phillip was holding was green. When I jumped on that limb, it flung me into the air just like a springing diving board – right into the river! I felt like I was falling into a bucket of ice water. My first thoughts were of the numbing cold. Then I remembered that snapping turtle, and I climbed out of the water faster than I'd fallen in. When I landed on the bank, Dad, Phil and W.B. were rolling with laughter.

Dad and W.B. were obsessive fishermen and wouldn't leave the river under any circumstances. Dad, Phillip and I were on the river fishing another night while there were tornadoes around us. Dad had brought a portable radio with him so that we could listen to the weather report. The storms were all around us, and they were bad storms. Dad became a little concerned. He said, "Boys, if a tornado hits right here, I want you to lay in those bushes over there and grab the roots and hold on."

Like that would save us from a tornado. We had our safety plan in place, so we weren't about to leave the river.

Another time, I spent the night at Phil's house and we stayed out much later than we were supposed to. Uncle W.B. was angry, and when he heard us walk onto the front porch, he was waiting for us. Phil unlocked the front door, and I stepped in front of him, walking into the house. Just as I did, W. B. swung a 1 x 2 hardwood bed slat, striking me in the head. The impact knocked me to the floor.

W.B. saw that it was I instead of Phillip that he had knocked down. "I didn't mean to hit you. I thought you were Phillip," he said.

I had felt the wrath of Uncle W.B., but it was nothing compared to Aunt Reubene's anger after she caught Phillip and me in the basement bedroom with a couple of girls. Late one night, Phillip, two teenage girls and I crawled in through a basement bedroom window. The four of us were lying on the bed in the dark room, fully clothed trying to be quiet. We were talking and laughing and we woke up Aunt Reubene. You would have thought we had murdered someone and buried then in the basement when she caught us with those girls there. She scolded us and got W.B. out of bed to drive the girls home.

I was a failure in school, and a young punk with a chip on my shoulder. By the time I was 15, I had been picked up for assault and was in jail for car theft.

My cousin, Phil, and Danny Taylor were my two best friends and constant companions. We walked around on Friday and Saturday nights, and searched until we found an old 1955 or '56 Chevrolet. You could start those vehicles without the key if the ignition switch wasn't locked. When we found one unlocked, we would hop in and drive around for several hours and then return the car where we found it. One night, Danny and a couple of other guys got caught in a stolen car. They were arrested and put in jail.

They were nice enough to let the police know that I also had also been with them on other occasions. The police called my house on a Sunday morning and told my mother to ask me to come by the police station so that they could talk to me. When I arrived, the police asked me if I had ever been with the guys when they stole a car. I admitted that I had been.

There wasn't any evidence against me. I wasn't with the guys the night before, and there wasn't a complaint against me. However, I was arrested at age 15 and put in jail for about a week. I had to go before a judge, who put me on probation for a year and suspended me from getting a driver's license until I was 17.

One night, I took my dad's car keys, and my cousin Phillip and I pushed Dad's car down the street where he wouldn't hear me start it. We started the car and drove off. A couple of hours later, my grandfather, who was visiting from Alabama, became very ill and needed to be taken to the hospital. My dad and grandfather walked outside to get into the car to go to the hospital and – surprise – there was no car there. Fortunately, they got him to the hospital, where he improved and was soon released. Dad definitely let me know what he thought about my shenanigans.

While in the seventh grade, I once spent the night with Danny Taylor. Larry Freeman, his older cousin, was a three-time local Golden Gloves champion, and he lived next door to Danny. They were from the same area of Mississippi that we were from. Danny and I walked to Larry's house and we went into Larry's bedroom. Larry wasn't at home so Danny opened Larry's closet to show me three beautiful Delong letter jackets with a huge boxing glove on them and the words "Golden Gloves Champion" embroidered on them.

This fired Danny and me up. We couldn't wait until we were 16 so we could compete in the Golden Gloves. Larry was about eight years older than us, and he took Danny and me to the boxing gym. Danny was a year older, so he began boxing a year before me.

I went to the gym and was the timekeeper that year. Danny boxed for about four months because Larry was a fanatical trainer, and he made Danny run 10 to 12 miles with him every day. After competing that year in the Golden Gloves, Danny quit boxing. Larry literally ran Danny away from the sport by making him train so hard. World champions, when training for world title fights, rarely run more than five miles per day.

Since Larry and Danny lived about 10 miles away from me, I occasionally would join them for one of their marathon runs. When I began competing as an amateur boxer, Larry was drafted into the army and went to Vietnam.

I did roadwork on my own. I would run three to five miles a day to prepare for a three-round bout instead of Larry's bizarre routine.

Once I learned how to box, I noticed it was very easy to abuse someone in a fight who didn't have any formal training. For a little while, in my teenage years, I took advantage of this and hurt a few individuals. In spite of all the trouble I got into, I was never a mean person. I was always a softhearted guy, and other than a few occasions when I punched someone without being provoked, I used the knowledge I had gained in boxing to defend myself and not to abuse anyone else. I also learned that if you went looking for trouble, you could find more than you wanted. However, boxing did give me a lot of self-confidence and a little bit of an attitude for years.

Boxing always has been the poor man's sport. When there were many poor Irishman who migrated to America, there were many good Irish boxers. The same can be said for the Italians, African-Americans and Mexicans as well. A young man from a well-to-do family doesn't have to fight for a living. It's much too hard. There are so many other opportunities for him. But for the poor, boxing has been a way out of poverty, crime and a wayward life. Boxing has helped many young men by providing them an outlet to vent anger and frustration in a controlled environment. It also has helped many poor youngsters move out of drug-invested ghettos. The great lightweight champion Roberto Duran ate from a garbage can as a youngster in his native Panama before he became rich and famous as a boxer. George Foreman rose from abject poverty in the mean streets of Houston and even Oscar De La Hoya escaped the gang-controlled streets of East Los Angeles all because of the sport of boxing. James J. Braddock, boxing's "Cinderella Man," was actually on welfare before he secured a fight for and won the world heavyweight championship in the 1930s. Each champion became wealthy as a result of the much-maligned sport of boxing.

Boxing has helped not only these famous champions but countless other poor kids who have used the sport as a positive outlet to learn discipline, self-esteem and the value of hard work.

Uncle Grady

Larry Broughman, Larry Freeman and my Uncle Grady were my first heroes. Larry and Grady were cool guys who rode motorcycles. Larry a BSA and Grady and my cousin, J.T., rode Triumphs. BSA, Norton and Triumph were the cool bikes in the 1960s. Harley hogs were fat and ugly until motorcycle gangs like the Hell's Angels started to strip them down.

Broughman, Freeman, Uncle Grady and J.T were tough guys you didn't push around. Since I had been pushed around for most of my life, I had an insatiable desire to be one of the tough guys.

Uncle Grady was six years older than me. When he graduated from high school in Alabama in 1962, he moved to Kenosha and got a job at American Motors. Grady loved to drink and hang out in the local bars. He and the others rode their motorcycles, and they would fight anybody, at anytime.

One night Grady and Larry Freeman were in a tavern. There was a big, cocky guy from Kenosha who got into a fight and was whipping one of the southern boys that night. He hollered out for everyone to hear: "I'll whup (sic) you and all of your hillbilly friends."

Then they all walked outside and Grady said, "Let me put my coat in the car and I'll fight you."

Grady went to his car and slipped on brass knuckles. He walked to the big guy and hit him on the jaw, knocking him down and out in the street.

Larry Freeman was also someone who wouldn't back down or turn his back on anyone who wanted to fight. Freeman wasn't a big guy, but he was unnaturally fearless. He would fight man or beast. He was about 5-foot-8 and boxed as a lightweight at 135 pounds. When he wasn't boxing, he weighed about 160 pounds.

Fight The Good Fight

There was a fellow by the name of Ed who had won the Kenosha Golden Gloves tournament as a heavyweight. He was a big bully who weighed more than 300 pounds. One day he got into an argument with Freeman at a local garage. Ed tried to bully Freeman and they started scuffling. Ed grabbed Freeman by the throat and almost choked him unconscious. Larry was pinned against a counter and reached for something to stop Ed from choking him to death. His hand located a ball peen hammer on the counter behind him. He grasped the hammer, hit the behemoth and knocked him unconscious.

On another evening, Larry and Danny were in a tavern and obviously had had too much to drink. Larry got into an argument about a pool game with another man who was about 6-foot-6 tall and weighed about 250 pounds. They went outside the bar and began to fight.

Larry and his adversary were wrestling around, and Larry was hollering instructions at Danny.

"Hit him Danny ... hit him Danny."

Every time Danny threw a punch to hit the huge target, the big man would lift Larry into the air as a shield. Danny would hit Larry by accident instead of his intended target. Danny and the big man were beginning to really hurt ol' Larry. He desperately needed help. Fortunately for Larry, the police arrived, and not a minute too soon. They quickly stopped the assault.

Someone Cared For Me

First Assembly of God in Kenosha was a great church with tremendous men of God who ministered to my family.

Wally Block, a Christian businessman, was my Sunday school teacher. Wally was a great inspiration to me. He showed true Christian love to me while I was a teenager. He would come by my house and take me to lunch and encourage me. The summer that I turned 16, he offered to help pay my way to church camp.

I made a profession of faith in Christ at that camp in Waupaca, Wisconsin. I attempted to live a Christian life for a few months, but I continued to run around with my old friends. John Wilkerson was our pastor. He is the uncle of David Wilkerson, the author of *The Cross and the Switchblade* and the founder of Teen Challenge, a Christian treatment center for drug addicts. Rich Wilkerson, John's son, was a good friend to me. Today, he is a well-known pastor and evangelist. Dick Eastman, another well-known author and evangelist, was our youth pastor.

Dick spent many months trying to help me – a troubled, wounded and confused teenager – to find direction in life. He was prepping me for the ministry. He had me speak in front of church audiences as we traveled with a youth choir. He also took me to speak to residents in nursing homes.

In the fall, I started running around with an old friend from my pre-Christian days. While we were hanging out on the street corner, a girl came by whom I had dated and had had a physical relationship with. My old friend started enticing me, saying, "Wouldn't you like to be with her again?"

After I had spent several of the best months of my life serving the Lord, I yielded to my fleshly desires and to his suggestion. I sinned, so I felt that I had failed as a Christian. From that point, I felt too guilty to return to church, and I

Fight The Good Fight

went deeper and deeper into sin. I spent the next four years of my life floundering and getting into much more trouble.

"My son, if sinners entice you, do not consent." (Proverbs 1:10) I didn't heed wise instruction, and I believe I missed my calling in life. At that time in my life I felt the Lord was leading me into ministry, but I failed. Who knows what God had in store for me had I been obedient. If God is leading you to do something big or even spectacular, then I would encourage you to attack it with all of your might. Have blinders on, and don't veer to the right hand or the left, but stay focused, obedient and true, and complete what God has purposed you do. I don't know why, but almost everyone will tell you that you can't do it. But if God has given you a desire to do something, you can do it.

Live Fast! Die Young

At 17, I was hanging out with a group of bikers older than me who were "wanna be" Hell's Angels. One spring night, we broke into a gas station and took the money in the cash register. There was only about $20 in the register, but it was enough to buy all of us something to eat.

Afterward, we stopped at a local Italian restaurant. It's funny how you remember certain things. That was many years ago, but I remember ordering spaghetti and meatballs and the waiter telling me they were out of meatballs and he would have to substitute sausage. Someone put a quarter in the jute box and I remember hearing 1960s British pop music icon Tom Jones sing "The Green, Green Grass of Home."

The other guys were disappointed that we didn't have enough cash for a beer party on the beach of Lake Michigan that night, so they decided that we should break into another gas station to get some money to buy the beer. Donnie, a local thug, was behind the wheel as we drove north on 7th Avenue and reached the intersection at Sheridan Road, we spotted another gas station that was closed.

Colin, who was five years older than me, spoke up and said, "Pull in there! Let's hit that one."

He was riding shot-gun in the front seat and even though there were five of us in the car and I was the youngest, he turned around and looked at me in the back seat and said, "Kerry, you're going with me aren't you?"

I really didn't want to go, so I responded with a grunt, "uh?"

"You're not scared are you?" he asked. I was scared, but what could I say? "No man, I ain't scared! I'll go with you."

We got out of the car and the other guys drove away. We walked to the south side of the station and smashed a window in the garage bay. I walked to the front of the building to make sure that we were in the clear before we crawled inside the window. Just as I peeped around the building, I noticed a police car approximately 100 yards away with officers coming our way.

"Hey Colin, here come the cops. We better run!" I hollered.

We ran behind the gas station onto a field. I was much faster than Colin and had raced 25 yards ahead of him. Suddenly, he stopped and lay down in the weeds to hide from the police. I kept running as fast as I could. After running about two blocks, I came to a side street. Immediately after I ran out of the field, I glanced to my left. Bearing down on me at a high rate of speed was a police car. The car was coming so fast that I couldn't get away.

The car was on me in an instant. The officers stopped the car and jumped out with their pistols drawn, grabbed me and threw me onto the car. They slapped handcuffs on me and placed me under arrest. They positioned me in the back seat of the car and as they drove south on Sheridan Road toward the police station, I glanced to my right and noticed a car had pulled up beside us. It was our three other partners in crime who had stayed in the car while Colin and I did the dirty work. They glanced at me, and I coolly nodded to them as they drove by.

I got out of this scrape with the law because I was a juvenile and I didn't tell the police officers anything about my older accomplices. Colin got away because he had hidden in the field behind the gas station.

Several years later, Colin and Corky, a former Golden Gloves champion that I knew from the boxing gym, were riding on their motorcycles. They were going about five miles above the speed limit when they passed a parked police car. The police car pulled onto the road behind them, turned on their squad car lights and motioned for Colin and Corky to stop on the right side. Instead of stopping and facing the insignificant consequences of their speeding, they gunned the throttle on their motorcycles and tried to outrun the police. They reached speeds of more than 100 miles an hour as they tried to get away, not knowing that a police roadblock awaited them.

They tried to go around the roadblock, but there was no escape. Colin was a big guy and his motorcycle went airborne. Colin slammed into a telephone pole and was impaled by a spike on that pole. Colin died from massive facial injuries and Corky was crippled for life. Colin had gambled with his life and lost. He was 31 when he died.

I was involved in crime with these men when I was a boy because I wanted to fit in. I wanted to be accepted and to be part of their clique.

During my teenage years, I would do and try almost anything. If someone dared me to do something, no matter how crazy or bizarre it was, I would attempt it. I was a self-destructive person who was always doing stupid and illegal things without contemplating or caring about the consequences of my actions. Some people said that I was brain-dead; some said that I was crazy or full of the devil. Others believed I was incorrigible. Because of my wild and crazy behavior as a teenager, my mother and grandmother told me I needed psychiatric help. I did many things that I regret today.

Trying to belong or to fit in or to be somebody is how I first became involved in alcohol, drugs and crime. I never liked the taste of beer or wine, but found myself as a teenager standing in an alley chugging a bottle of Muscatel wine because the other guys wanted to get drunk. I didn't want them to know that I hated the taste of booze.

I didn't care anything about drugs, but because my peers were doing drugs, I felt obligated to do the same. It began with smoking marijuana, then snorting cocaine. Later,

I almost fried my brain on amphetamines. It all began as casual drug use.

My buddies and I would take speed and stay up for days at a time, not sleeping or eating anything. After we stopped taking the speed our bodies would crash, and many times it felt like suffering through a car wreck. It was very painful and hard on the body. I also had a very bad trip on LSD or acid. I had a scary hallucination about hell. When I did drugs or drank alcohol, the little social etiquette or inhibitions I possessed went out the window. I would do or say almost anything. I had a vile, venomous mouth that constantly spewed out foul, filthy cursing.

Because I was unwilling to do homework in school, I saw that I was going to flunk a class in 10th grade. I knew that I wouldn't be able to play football the next year. I went to the teacher of that class and asked him to allow me to do make-up work so that I wouldn't fail. He said no. I was a failure in school, I was a failure in life and I had failed miserably as a Christian.

I went across the street to the courthouse where the Marine Corps recruiter had an office. I told him my situation and he assured me that I could play football in the Marine Corps. Ha, ha. So I quit school and told the recruiter I would come back and enlist as soon as I turned 17 in July. After my birthday on July 4, I joined the Marine Corps on the two-year enllstment program. My parents had to sign the papers because I was underage.

I had a great amount of difficulty getting accepted by the Marine Corps after I had enlisted. I had studied so little in the years I was in school that I barely passed the entrance exam. I barely passed and scored one point above a failing grade. I was one point from being classified as a moron. At first, the Marines weren't going to accept me because of the trouble I already had been in with the law. I met with an officer to get his approval to let me enlist. He did.

Six weeks after I turned 17, I was in boot camp in San Diego, California. Again, I was always in trouble even when I wasn't trying to be. In boot camp, you are given every kind of physical exam. While in the dental office a Naval dental assistant was going to take an X-ray of my teeth, so he tried to place a bitewing holder in my mouth. He became enraged when I gagged on it. He hatefully cursed me and said, "I'll make you swallow this thing."

Then he tried to force it into my mouth, causing me to gag even worse. (After I left the Marine Corps, I purposely picked fights with sailors on leave in Kenosha from Great Lakes Naval Academy about 30 miles away. Somehow I felt I was getting even with the dental assistant.)

A few days later while our platoon was in marching formation, I happened to look at one of my drill instructors. This was a no-no.

"What are you looking at? You slimy homo!" he screamed at me.

As if that wasn't degrading and insulting enough, he had a magazine rolled up in his hand that he used as a club, smashing it across my face.

Several weeks later, another Marine was talking while we were standing at attention in the chow line. I said. "Shhhhh! You're going to get us into trouble."

A different drill instructor than the one who hit me with the magazine heard our conversation and said, "I'll see you two in my office after chow."

After lunch, the drill instructor called us into his office in one of the Quonset huts. He was a little sadistic, muscular man, standing 5-foot-5. As punishment, he had us stand and face each other in front of him. He then ordered us to punch each other while we were standing there. Each time we threw a punch I had the advantage against my fellow Marine because I knew a little more about throwing punches. Every time I hit him, I would knock him across the room while his

Fight The Good Fight

punches didn't move me. I was beginning to enjoy this little game we were playing and I started to laugh out loud. That was a big mistake. The drill instructor wasn't laughing.

"So you think this is funny huh?" he said.

"Sir, No sir!" I replied.

"Let me show you what's funny," he said.

He punched me as hard as he could in the solar plexus, knocking the breath out of me. Since I took that shot so well – I only was gasping for air and trying to breathe, but I had the audacity to still be standing – he continued to hit me until I buckled over. Evidently, this was the drill instructors' modus operandi, because there was another marine in our platoon who was a huge bodybuilder with thick abdominal muscles that included an impressive six-pack.

The fellow Marine got into trouble with this same drill instructor, who told him, "I'll break that crust of yours."

He proceeded to hit him in the stomach until he had placed bruises all over the Marine's abdomen. The next day, his stomach muscles were swollen from the drill instructor's beating. I learned my lessons. I never looked at the drill instructor again, and I didn't talk while in the chow line, either.

After I was discharged from the Marines two years later, I returned to Kenosha. Once home, I began hanging out with my old buddies.

I was 19 in November when my friend, Danny Taylor, and I got this crazy idea to hitch hike to California. We were going to go there to become movie stars. Danny was a really cool guy. He was the coolest guy I ever knew. But in those days, I believe we were about as bright as Lenny and Squiggy were from the old *La Vergne and Shirley* television series. We began hitchhiking late one evening. After a tough four or five days on the road, we arrived in Los Angeles.

We stayed in a hotel the first night. After that, we bummed around Hollywood for about a week until we were almost out of money. We stayed on the street or in "hippy crash pads" because we had nowhere else to go.

We contemplated looking for jobs and staying in L.A., but Danny had been charged with a felony before we left Wisconsin. He had been caught with a sawed-off shotgun in his possession. He was scheduled to be in federal court in Milwaukee about two weeks later. We decided we should head home so he wouldn't miss his trial. We started hitch-hiking, and before we got very far down the road, Danny was able to score a nickel bag of marijuana from a young man who had given us a ride.

After several hours of hitchhiking, we were east of Los Angeles near San Bernardino. It was dark, and while we were standing on the side of the road, a man in his early 20s and driving a pickup truck stopped to give us a ride. There were two young children in the truck with him. One of the children was a toddler no more than 2; the other was a baby just a few months old. He said he had room for one of us in the cab and there was a sleeping bag in the bed of the truck where the other could ride. Since we hadn't had a lot of sleep in the last 10-plus days, Danny volunteered to climb in the back and sleep.

I rode in the truck with the man and the children. I thought it was strange for him to be alone with just the children. I asked him the whereabouts of their mother. He told me she was a no-good tramp, and he had left her and had taken the children. He said that he was headed home to North Carolina. I said, "That's great; we'll ride to Tennessee with you and hitchhike to Wisconsin from there."

He said he was broke, but he was a gambler. He asked if we would mind riding north with him to Las Vegas, where he could gamble and win some money. I told him that sounded great. Off we went.

He had a loaf of bread and a package of bologna in the truck, and he told me to help myself to it. So he and I talked

Fight The Good Fight

and ate bologna sandwiches all the way to Vegas while the children and Danny slept. It was about 2 a.m. when we arrived. He stopped the truck in a vacant lot and reached behind the seat and pulled out a .38-caliber pistol.

He said, "I'm going to go into town and get some money. "Will you watch the kids?" Obviously I didn't want to leave those kids alone, and I didn't want to say no to a man holding a .38-caliber pistol.

I replied, "Yes, I will."

After he left, I got out of the truck and walked to the back to wake Danny. I told him what had happened. We both knew the man was looking for: someone to rob.

"What should we do?" Danny asked

"Man, we can't leave these babies here alone," I said. "We'll just have to wait until he returns."

Danny agreed. We sat there until almost daylight when the children's father finally returned.

"I wasn't able to get any money, but I've got some friends up north in Idaho," he said. "Would you like to go with me?"

Simultaneously, we said, "No, man. That's OK. We'll get out here in Vegas."

Because of our diversion to Las Vegas, we were six hours north of I-40, the highway we were traveling home on. We started hitchhiking toward home. We were south of Las Vegas, a few miles from Hoover Dam when off in the distance we could see a highway patrol car. We knew hitchhiking was illegal in Nevada, so we turned around and began walking down the highway. The patrol car got about 100 yards in front of us, then the patrolman slammed on his brakes and started backing up. Very quickly, Danny threw the bag of marijuana away that he had bought the day before.

The patrolman got to where we were standing and rolled down his window. He said, "Get in. I'll give you a ride."

We climbed into the car and rode with him for 50 miles. While riding along, he told us we were very fortunate not to

57

Fight The Good Fight

have been hitchhiking while he came by or he would have arrested us and taken us to jail. I thought to myself, *"Yeah, we're really lucky you didn't see Danny throw the marijuana away."* Go figure. If we had stuck our thumbs out, indicating we wanted a ride, we would have been put in jail. But since we didn't hitchhike, he was giving us a ride.

Later that day, we made it to I-40 somewhere near Kingman, Arizona. We stood on the interstate and held our thumbs out for several hours in front of a gas station, but no one stopped to pick us up. We hadn't shaven or taken a bath in several days, so I'm sure we looked frightful. We purchased a razor and bathed and shaved in the gas station restroom sink. A short time later, a young man stopped and gave us a ride. It was now my turn to lie down and sleep, so I stretched out in the back seat of the car. The last thing I remember the driver saying before I drifted off to sleep was that he was going to Kansas.

A couple of hours later, Danny abruptly awakened me. Since I hadn't slept in a couple of days, I was in a deep, almost trancelike sleep. I struggled to awaken as Danny opened the back door of the car. Suddenly I felt a blast of artic air.

"Come on Kerry, we're getting out here," Danny said.

I staggered out of the car into the freezing night air. I asked Danny why we had gotten out of the car when the driver said he was going to Kansas. Danny said that the driver was stopping to get a motel room so he stopped and let us out to continue hitchhiking. When the driver had picked us up, it wasn't that cold. Now it felt as though we had been dropped off at the North Pole. It was snowing and it was bitterly cold.

"Danny where are we?" I asked.

"I don't know," he replied.

We walked down the highway about 50 yards where we saw a sign that said Flagstaff. Instantly, it hit me that we were in the Flagstaff, Arizona, mountains.

Fight The Good Fight

We walked from the interstate to town. We had about $4 between us, and we walked to every cheap hotel in town trying to find someone who would give us shelter from the cold night air. No one would give us a room for $4. Finally, a night manager at one of the hotels told us where to find a boarding house. We walked to the address he gave us and entered a glass-enclosed front porch. There was no heat on the front porch, but there were two twin beds. We knocked on the door to the house. A lady came to the door and cracked it open as we told her our situation and offered her our last four dollars for shelter. She took the money and said, "You can sleep on the front porch." She then closed and locked the front door to the house.

Danny and I were pretty well beaten up by life and our current circumstances at this point. We were cold, hungry, tired and weary. Even though there was no heat on that front porch, we were thankful for a place to sleep and re-energize. That night we both decided we had had enough of the type of life we were living. We agreed we were going to return home, get a job and begin to live a normal life. We fell asleep. When we awakened the next morning, we walked to a pawnshop, where we pawned both of our watches to get money for breakfast and to make a phone call home. I called my dad, who wired me enough money to catch a bus home. Danny called his cousin Larry, who did the same for him.

Danny made it back in time for the federal court hearing. The charges against him subsequently were dropped. Danny eventually settled down and married Pam Radley, his long-time girlfriend. They started a family and had two children, Steven and Jamie, who now are grown. Sadly, we lost Danny to throat cancer in 1989. I'm certain I'll see him in heaven because he also gave his life to Jesus Christ several years before he died.

Cruising Main Street with Diane Smith

After arriving home from our California trip, I got my first job as a salesman at a local shoe store. I soon got a car. Several months, later my cousin Phil and I were standing on the corner in downtown Kenosha. It was cruising night. There were hundreds of teenagers cruising Main Street.

Diane Smith and her friend Shirley Maxedon drove by. They waved and said hello. I was grown up now and I didn't look like the scruffy little boy from the trailer park. I was dressed nicely, and I'd been told I was a handsome young man. I asked them to stop and let us ride with them. When they stopped, Phil and I got in the back seat.

Diane was driving. I leaned over the seat and said, "Diane, I've always wanted to go out with you."

"You have?" she said, smiling

"Yes," I replied, and asked her what she was doing Saturday night.

"I've got plans this Saturday," she said.

"How about next Saturday?" I asked.

She tried to act cool and said nothing. I asked her if she would go out with me and she said yes.

Diane was a beautiful young Christian lady. She was very pretty on the outside, but was even more beautiful on the inside. She was everything I had ever dreamed about in a wife. I literally fell in love with her when I first met her as a child in the trailer court. Even though I was a moral dirt bag, I knew the priceless value of a Christian lady who didn't drink, curse or smoke.

Once I began dating her, I left my old friends and was on my best behavior. My cousin Phil jokes today that after we got into her car that night, he never saw me again. Diane was the epitome of a lady, full of charm and grace. I admired and respected her Christian character and conduct. After we married, she encouraged me to go to church with her.

Reluctantly I did occasionally go. Very slowly, my life began to change.

Diane was one of the most dynamic Christian people I've known in my life. I'm sure living with me was very difficult for her. She deserved someone much better than I was for many years of our marriage. She had a great moral compass, and she always let me know when I was off-course, which was most of the time. God used her sweet, gentle Christian spirit to convict me of my sin and, ultimately, to change my behavior.

I was working and I had gotten my GED. I started taking courses at a local community college and the University of Wisconsin-Parkside.

One source of irritation for Diane was my obsessive love for boxing. I would drive to Milwaukee almost every day to spar with a couple of local professional boxers, Vidal Flores and Stanley Moore. She hated the sport. When I would box, she stayed at home because she didn't want to see me fight. Since I was sparring with professional boxers, I got my attitude adjusted and my butt kicked every day for about six months before I started holding my own. One day while she washed the blood out of my gym clothes, she began crying and asked me why I continued to box. She didn't understand how much I needed boxing to make me feel good about myself.

I loved it. After sparring many rounds in the ring for more than 10 years, I only felt pain twice. The first time was in an amateur boxing match when I hit an opponent with a wild left hook that broke my thumb. The second time was while sparring with Lamont Lovelady, who hit me with a clean shot and broke my nose. Lovelady was a National Golden Gloves Champion who punched much harder than his last name suggested.

As I took on the responsibilities of a husband and later as a father, I got a job as a traveling salesman, which kept me on the road during the week. I did this for several years and it interfered with my goal of becoming a professional boxer. Basically, I became a weekend gym rat and a sparring partner for the pros instead of becoming a professional boxer myself.

My job soon transferred me to Des Moines, Iowa. While there, I trained with professional boxers Art and Dale Hernandez and Lovelady. Art was a world rated middleweight and the North American Boxing Federation middleweight champion, Dale was a world-class lightweight and Lamont was a national champion as a middleweight. I learned good boxing technique while training with the pros. This experience allowed me to later start a boxing team and teach young men how to box.

I once was offered $75 for a four-round professional boxing match against a very good fighter when his opponent didn't show up for the bout. This was in the early 1970s, but it wasn't a very enticing offer to fight a killer, so I passed on this not-so-great opportunity.

God Gave Us Christy

Even though I had married a Christian woman, my heart still was desperately wicked. I wouldn't do drugs, drink alcohol or anything bad around her. But when I was away from her, I would. Four years after we married, we had a precious daughter that we named Christy. When Christy was a baby and was sitting in her high chair, I looked at her and thought to myself, *"How is she ever going to have a chance to go to heaven with a father like you?"*

That thought impacted me so deeply I decided to give my life totally to Jesus Christ and raise that little girl in a Christian home. I struggled as a Christian and with sin that had me in its grip for several more years. I was a weak Christian who was attracted to the material things of this world, and I backslid and failed again, again and again.

Theologian Robert L. "Bob" Deffenbaugh, teacher and elder at Community Bible Church in Richardson, Texas, has written "salvation brings immediate forgiveness for sin, but not immediate freedom from sin."

Sadly, that described my Christian walk.

The difference was that, instead of chasing after sinful things as I had in the past, I now ran from those things or avoided them. I no longer went to those old places or hung out with those people who would entice me to do wrong. God in his mercy saved me and changed my lifestyle and, ultimately, my life. Later, I moved our small family to Tennessee to attend Tennessee Temple University, a Baptist Bible college.

Although I've sinned too many times to count and I have failed in many things in my life, failure isn't final with God. I've given my life to Christ and he has forgiven me of my past. I can't go back and rewrite the things I've done wrong. But my future is secure because I've placed my trust in Christ.

Fight The Good Fight

"Although you can't go back and make a new beginning, you can start now and make a new ending," said Carl Bard.

"Failure is an event, not a person," Zig Ziglar, nationally known author and motivational speaker, said.

As long as you are willing to get up and keep moving after being knocked down failure isn't final. The late Col. Harlan Sanders, founder of Kentucky Fried Chicken, wasn't a big success until he was a senior citizen. He had failed many times in life but eventually became monumentally successful.

Chapter 3: My Boxers

Courage through the Fire

Loud music began to play as the great boxing champion Thomas "Hit Man" Hearns and his entourage began making their way to the boxing ring that had been assembled in the center of the 50,000-seat Aloha Stadium in Honolulu, Hawaii. The five-time world champion had feasted on many an opponent in his celebrated career. He had knocked out contenders like world champions Pipino Cuevas and Dennis Andries, and even KO'd the legendary champion Roberto Duran in the second round of a title fight in his illustrious career. He had outboxed the wondrous Wilfredo Benitez, the youngest man ever to win a world boxing title, and had nearly stopped the great Sugar Ray Leonard in their first encounter. The mere mention of Hearns' name made world-class boxers weak in the knees.

Ken "The Bull" Atkin of Smyrna, Tennessee, who was an unknown and unheralded boxer that I managed and trained throughout his career, already was gloved and waiting in the ring to face the famous boxer. Keith McKnight, another one of my boxers, and I were standing in the ring with Atkin as Hearns and his entourage made their way toward the boxing ring. Atkin was brought in to be Hearns' next sacrificial lamb in his quest for another world title.

Atkin had started late in boxing at age 19. He'd had a very limited amateur career of only 12 bouts. He wasn't as skillful and polished as the boxers who had extended amateur careers. But he was extremely tough and he was one of the most courageous guys I ever worked with. He had been nicknamed "The Bull" in junior high school because of his ram-charging ways.

Atkin's dream of having a shot at the big-time came the day boxing promoter Harold Smith called me looking for an opponent for Hearns. In boxing, the word "opponent" doesn't have good connotations. An opponent isn't brought in to win. He is someone who is brought in to give a great fighter some work. Oftentimes, opponents are nothing more than washed up tomato cans – used to build up the record of his adversary. Smith even asked me on the telephone before the fight. "You're not going to bring your guy in and upset my fighter are you?"

Even though we were going to do everything in our power to win, I didn't want to say anything that might cause Smith to find another opponent for Hearns. So I said, "Harold, you know the odds of us beating Hearns are slim to none." He chuckled and that was the end of that conversation.

Our strategy was to play the opponent role right up until the bell rang. We were hoping that Hearns would take Atkin for granted and not train for the bout, thereby giving Ken his best chance of winning.

Unknown boxers who haven't won national amateur titles or competed at the Olympic level might get one or two opportunities in their careers, if they are lucky, to make it into big-time boxing. Many don't ever receive any big opportunities. Less than two percent of professional boxers make the multi-million paydays we read about in the newspaper. An "opportunity fight" such as this one is what the unknown,

Fight The Good Fight

underdog fighter fictionalized in the "Rocky" movies dreams about. If and when that opportunity comes, the underdog fighter jumps at the chance.

Atkin didn't see himself as an opponent. He saw himself as a winner instead of a loser. He wasn't afraid or intimidated of Hearns. He saw this as an opportunity of a lifetime and he trained like a man possessed. Boxers generally prepare for a 10-round fight by getting five miles of roadwork per day. Instead, Atkin ran eight or 10 miles per day in preparation for the April showdown with "The Hit Man, "also known as the "Motor City Cobra." Atkin went 15 rounds against several rugged sparring partners three times a week, even though the fight only was scheduled for 10 rounds.

Hearns was set to face Virgil Hill for the light–heavy-weight championship later in the year. As we stood in the ring we could see the "Hit Man" and his entourage at the far end of the stadium. They looked like an army coming toward us in the ring. The group was bouncing to the music, and everyone with Hearns was hollering at the champ encouraging him on.

Atkin had no entourage and no fans. It was just he, I and Keith McKnight standing in the corner. It felt like we were alone and outnumbered at a dog fight. Hearns was a vicious pit bull who had a platoon of antagonists on his side, pointing in our direction hollering, "Sic 'em!"

The group entered the ring like a military assault squad. The champion ran up the steps, climbed through the ropes and entered the boxing ring to the sound of thunderous applause. Like the maestro he was, he skillfully glided around the ring while glaring at Atkin. Suddenly Hearns twirled around, his regal robe swirling. His entire entourage was clapping, hollering instructions and encouragement to the champion with all of their eyes fixed on our corner. I thought: "*I hope I haven't made a mistake in matching Atkin with Hearns. I hope 'The Hit Man' doesn't hurt my fighter.*"

Then I said a silent prayer for my friend. Atkin completely was oblivious to this psychological warfare and snapped me out of my somber reflection when he turned to me with a smile and asked, "What? Is all of that supposed to scare me or something?"

The anxiety and nervousness you feel as a boxer, trainer or manager in the ring before a big fight is extremely intense. Butterflies swirl in your stomach and your mind runs a hundred miles an hour as you wonder what is about to happen. Amazingly, once the bell sounds for the fight to begin, you relax and your nerves become calm.

Boxers usually start the bout in a feeling-out process. They meet in the center of the ring and begin testing each other, probing for openings or weaknesses in the opponent. Many boxing matches don't become competitive or intense for a round or two. We threw that strategy out the window in the bout with Hearns. I felt that the safest place for Atkin in his bout against Hearns was on his chest. Atkin trained to crowd Hearns, and to fight him inside.

Just before the bell sounded for the first round to begin, I told Atkin, "You've got 10 seconds to get on his chest."

The courageous 5-foot-7 Atkin showed no respect for Hearns, his power or his reputation; he ran across the ring and jumped on the 6 foot 1 inch champion's chest and drew the champion into a brawl. Hearns backed into a neutral corner, then maneuvered his head to Atkin's left shoulder, artfully sliding his body to the other side of Atkin where he dug three ferocious left hooks deep into Atkin's midsection. This would have crushed many boxers, but Atkin was in the best shape of his life and the punches didn't seem to faze him.

Former World Welterweight Champion Carlos Palomino was the television color commentator sitting at ringside calling the fight. "Boy, this Atkin kid is tough! He doesn't believe he is an opponent. He came to win."

Fight The Good Fight

Hearns pivoted out of the corner and fired his piston-like jab at Atkin with the speed of a bullet. Swish! The jab snapped Atkin's head back. Atkin ducked the next shot Herms threw, and then he bulled the champion into the ropes, attempting to rough him up. Atkin then threw a picture-perfect right hand, his best shot of the fight, which landed squarely on Hearns' chin.

Palomino hollered, "Man, Atkin just hit Hearns with a really good shot!"

The punch sent Hearns into the ring ropes, where he balanced himself and covered up. The bell sounded, ending the first round.

As the second round began, Hearns turned up the heat. He fired thunderous punches at "the Bull," one after the other. Atkin rolled under most of the punches and moved forward, firing punches of his own. Tommy was trying to drill Atkin with that famous right hand, the same punch he had knocked out champions and legends with. But each time he threw the punch, Atkin employed a maneuver made famous by Detroit boxers, referred to as a shoulder roll, to get underneath the punch.

Fight The Good Fight

Ken "The Bull" Atkin goes toe-to-toe for three rounds with Thomas "Hit Man" Hearns in Hawaii.

For six minutes, "The Bull" battled Hearns on even terms, giving as much as he took. During the middle of the third round Atkin was hit above his left eye, opening a deep cut. The referee looked at the bloody Atkin and asked the ringside physician to look at the gash. The doctor advised the referee to stop the bout, which he did. Hearns was awarded a third-round technical knockout.

Later that year, Hearns went on to win the light-heavyweight world championship from Virgil Hill. Atkin later won the World Boxing Federation world light heavyweight championship. Hearns retired a multi-millionaire, while Atkin continued to work as a police officer in Smyrna throughout his career to pay his bills.

Fight The Good Fight

Atkin was a man who had the courage to compete with one of the greatest boxers in the sport's history. Very few people gave Atkin a chance to make it outside of the first round against Hearns. With such a tremendous disparity in skill and experience, Atkin wasn't supposed to be able to compete with Hearns. Though he didn't win the bout, he rose to the occasion and battled a great boxing champion on even terms for three rounds without getting knocked down or out. The heat was turned up and Atkin withstood the fire and didn't quit. Several weeks later, the great boxing champion graciously autographed a photo of himself and Atkin in the ring. On the photo, he wrote, "No Rematch, Thomas Hearns."

"Tyson's Gonna Knock You Out, Adam!"

Melvin Richards brought his son Adam to the boxing gym when he was only 8. The short, chubby kid didn't look very athletic. However, he had been raised to work hard and to "be tough." Because of his weight, there was no one his own age for him to spar. Given his size, he had to spar with older and more experienced boys. When he was in his early teens, we couldn't find anyone for him to box in his weight class, so he boxed exhibitions against grown men. He became tenacious, aggressive and very tough.

If someone got the best of him in a sparring session, he got angry. Sometimes he'd cry and then try to knock them out. He was a great youngster who always did what I asked of him. He was extremely polite and very tough mentally. He was willing to fight for what he believed in. I remember one instance where a young man in high school had made some obscene comments and really hurt a female classmate of Adam's. Adam quickly came to her defense and let the young offender know that if he hurt her again he would have to deal with him. He always seemed to be a friend to those who were defenseless.

I taught Adam how to box right handed even though he was a natural southpaw or lefthander like me. In boxing this is referred to as a converted southpaw. I had fought this way and knew that the boxers with the greatest left hooks were usually left-handed. I had also learned how to box this way and my best two punches were the left jab and left hook. When Adam was about 9 years old I said to him. "One day when you are older you will have a great left hook like Joe Frazier by fighting this way." I also taught him to throw the punch with all of his weight on his left foot and the palm of his hand facing vertically instead of horizontally with his wrist curled inward. The left hook is thrown several different

Fight The Good Fight

ways but I feel that this is the way to throw it with the most power.

Adam won two national championships at age 13 and 14 almost by default. In each of those years at the Silver Gloves, he only had to face one or two opponents. When he was 14, he was about 5-foot-5 and weighed more than 200 pounds. The summer of 1995, he competed at the National Junior Olympics and lost a decision to a Native American Indian boxer from Minnesota whose last name was Thunder. At 6-5, Thunder was about a foot taller than Adam.

At that point, Adam hadn't scored any knockouts. Rather, he won most of his bouts by decision. The next year, Adam, now 15, had grown to 6-1. His power had developed so much that he began knocking out every opponent he fought. His fearsome power carried him to the National Junior Olympics, as he knocked out every boxer he faced in the local and regional tournaments.

He had developed tremendous power, but his body composition was still soft and flabby. Everyone ignored Richards when he arrived at the Northern Michigan University campus in Marquette, Michigan, for the national championships. He won his first fight by knockout, but virtually no one noticed him. He didn't look like a fighter.

Instead, the kid capturing everyone's attention that year was a sculpted, muscular teenager, Leonard Childs. Childs and Richards were in the same weight class, but in different brackets. Childs, 16, resembled a full-fledged clone of "Iron" Mike Tyson, the youngest man to ever win the world heavyweight title and the so-called "baddest man on the planet." Childs won his first bout by knockout. Because of his power, his impressive physique and his physical resemblance to Tyson, everyone began to call him "Tyson." In the second round, Richards again knocked out his opponent, but so did Childs. Childs amazed everyone, but paid scant attention to Richards. They were on a collision course to meet in Saturday's finals, which would be nationally televised.

The media, fans and the other boxers all jumped on Childs' bandwagon. He looked so fearsome and impressive that it was easy to see why everyone was rallying around him. The other boxers in the tournament, including future Olympians Larry Mosley and Ricardo Williams, started badgering Adam, saying "Tyson's gonna knock you out, Adam." With a cruelty particular to teenagers, they kept repeating the chant. "Tyson's gonna knock you out, Adam … Tyson's gonna knock you out, Adam."

In the third round of the tournament, Adam knocked out another opponent. Childs faced Thunder, the big Minnesota kid who had beaten Adam the year before. Childs KO'd Thunder. After Childs' win, everybody fawned on him as if he was the real Mike Tyson – another prodigy destined to wreak havoc in the ring.

The cruel chants from the other boxers became much worse for Adam. The media representatives were excited because they thought they were witnessing the birth of another future professional champion in Leonard Childs. They built him up, swarming him while completely ignoring his opponent, Adam Richards.

I was with Adam that week, and I could see the pressure was enormously heavy for him. His peers, the fellow boxers in the tournament, believed he was going to get annihilated by Childs. Richards was scheduled to fight this seemingly invincible opponent in the Junior Olympic finals on national TV in just a couple of days.

This was merely an amateur boxing championship, not a professional world title. But I can't imagine any world champion experiencing any more pressure in a fight than what young Adam faced that week. I could see the tension in his face, as if he were fighting against the entire world. He was considered the underdog with no chance of winning. He was stressed and worried, but he wasn't about to give up. Adam didn't know the meaning of the word quit.

Babe Ruth, the great baseball player in the 1920s and '30s, once said, "It's hard to beat a person who never gives up." Adam was living proof of this Ruthian adage. His toughness and tenacity wouldn't allow him to consider quitting. He was going to face this challenge head on, man-to-man, in the boxing ring.

I tried to encourage him. I told him his instincts would kick in during the bout. I prayed with him and we asked the Lord to protect him and to help him perform to the best of his ability. I also told him everything would be OK once the bell rang.

I had watched Childs during every bout that week and knew Adam had a fighting chance. Although Childs was a very powerfully built young man with tremendous punching power, I knew that Adam was more experienced and sparred with professional boxers regularly in our gym. He also had developed a great left hook by this time and he was knocking boxers out cold with that punch. Quietly, I was confident that Adam would handle this challenge and emerge as the champion. When we arrived at the basketball arena where the bouts were being held on Saturday, Adam got dressed and I wrapped his hands. He loosened up, and we sat and watched the fighters in the lighter weight divisions compete in their championship bouts. After about two hours of waiting, the super-heavyweights finally were called to the glove table to have their gloves put on. When the Richards-Childs bout was called to the ring, Adam raced up the steps ready to face his adversary. I held the ropes open for him as he gladly stepped into that squared circle to fight.

When the bell sounded for the first round, Adam moved to the center of the ring to face Childs. After a brief feeling-out process, Adam threw his signature left hook, and caught Childs flush. Childs plummeted to the canvas and could not rise to his feet. Adam had knocked him out in the first minute of the first round with one single, explosive left hook.

How anticlimactic can you get? The fearsome-looking Childs ended up being no contest for Richards, who just had captured the national championship. He had knocked out every single person he faced in the District, Regional and National championships to do it. Wow! What an accomplishment for a shy, chubby 15-year-old.

Amazingly, Adam went on to win the national championship again in 1997 by again knocking out every opponent he faced. He co-holds the Junior Olympic record of winning the national heavyweight championship for two consecutive years and knocking out every opponent he faced. The only other person to accomplish this feat was none other than the real Mike Tyson, the youngest man to ever win the world heavyweight title.

Adam also won the Junior World Invitational tournament that same year, when he knocked out Dmitri Filimonov of Russia at 1-minute, 42 seconds of the first round.

One summer day after we returned home from the nationals, I gave Adam a ride home from the boxing gym. We got out of the car and goofed around in his front yard. We began wrestling each other. He was so strong that I had to work like crazy to make sure he didn't take me down. I was getting tired, but he wasn't!

Finally, we stopped our horseplay and both began laughing. I had escaped the wrestling match and had barely held my own with the 16-year-old Richards. I knew that in the next year or so he would be able to take me and throw me around like a beanbag, so I didn't wrestle him again. Soon, though, he started manhandling and bouncing everyone else around. Amateur boxers, professional boxers – it didn't matter; he was growing into manhood and had become a force to be reckoned with.

Fight The Good Fight

As his coach and mentor I always was treated with complete respect. That's just the way Adam was while I worked with him.

I worked with Adam in boxing for 11 years, from the very first day that he walked into the gym until he turned professional and had four pro bouts. Today he is a 240-pound, world-class professional. Adam recently served as a sparring partner for Evander "The Real Deal" Holyfield, the great four-time former heavyweight champion.

Adam was a joy to work with, and his courage and willingness to face a challenge no matter how tough will always be an inspiration to me. I watched him face the pressures of life head on. He's a champion at that, too. I wish him much success.

Tall, Talented Teen

I noticed a tall, skinny 17-year-old kid when he walked into our Middle Tennessee gym in the fall of 1989. He was almost impossible to notice, given that he stood 6-foot-6 and weighed 165 pounds.

"Hey, kid, what are you doing here?" I asked.

"I want to box," he replied.

I responded, "You must be kidding. These guys will break you in half in that boxing ring."

"No, I want to box," he said confidently.

He was so thin you would have thought he was the son of Popeye's girlfriend, Olive Oyl, from vintage cartoons. I really thought he was too thin to be a boxer. He got off to a shaky start against a smaller, more experienced boxer in his first amateur bout in Evansville, Indiana. But he developed into a very good amateur in his first year of boxing. Our amateur boxing team had become fairly successful and a local sports reporter called our gym Club Knockout. The boxers loved the moniker so we became the Club Knockout boxing team. Our original team included pugilists Ken "The Bull" Atkin, "Dangerous" Don Wilford and Tim "Scrap Iron" Johnson. These guys were all several years older than Keith (in fact they were grown men while he was still a teenager), and in the early days they roughed him up pretty good. But I could see the world-class talent in McKnight and knew that he would be something special when he matured. I figured he would be too big and skillful for my other boxers.

I saw both Keith's potential and his weaknesses early on in his development. I believed we could overcome those weaknesses and develop McKnight into a world champion. He won the Mid-State Golden Gloves three years consecutively, as well as the Spirit of America Championship for two consecutive years. He was also voted the Spirit of America's 1991 Best Boxer and Boxer of the Year.

Fight The Good Fight

At the Southern Golden Gloves championship in 1992, he faced future Olympian and heavyweight title challenger Calvin Brock. That night a talented but tentative Keith McKnight lost a decision to Brock. Brock told McKnight that he "thought he had received the decision over a more talented boxer." Having lost at the Southern Golden Gloves, he turned professional, although he was still very green and inexperienced.

Keith was a tremendously gifted athlete: tall, quick and mobile, with decent power. However, he had little self-confidence. I nurtured and protected him like he was my own son. I thought that we could groom him and develop him into a world champion.

'You've got to Knock Him Out to Win!'

As mentioned earlier, Keith McKnight arrived at my Middle Tennessee gym as a tall (6-foot-6), thin (165 pounds) 17-year-old. I introduced him to boxing, and trained him for eight years. I was his coach and trainer throughout his amateur days, and later shared those duties with several other trainers during his pro career. As an amateur, Keith compiled a 32-7 record and won numerous regional tournaments, including the Golden Gloves. When he turned pro, he grew to 220 pounds.

Keith is a very popular, good-natured young man. He loved to play practical jokes on others and he loved to laugh. Almost every day, he had a new joke to tell everyone. After he grew up, he worked for a bar and grill owned by his future father-in-law.

Keith had some hot sauce that was made from some of the hottest peppers in the world. The sauce was so hot that it would have been a good paint remover, and it was almost impossible to eat. He loved to bet people they couldn't eat his hot sauce. He always found some unsuspecting individual who thought they could eat anything. Keith would give them a taste of the hot sauce and, after tasting it, their face would turn blood red, and they would begin to gag and choke, drinking any liquid in sight to attempt to put out the sudden fire in their mouth and throat. McKnight would rear back and laugh his head off and say, "I tried to tell you it was too hot to eat."

McKnight would become one of the most graceful boxers you would ever see. He had tremendous God-given, athletic ability. He was blessed with height, speed and great coordination. He had quick hands and was very mobile and elusive. His only physical problem was that he was thin. Critics said he did not hit hard enough, that he lacked courage and he wasn't physically strong enough to compete as a premier heavyweight. Plus, he was white, and good, white heavyweight fighters were rare. Ever since the days of the great Jack Johnson, the first black man to win the world heavyweight title, people have been searching for the next "Great White Hope."

I remember watching Muhammad Ali in his prime on television and thinking he was thin. But, when I saw him in person for the first time, I was surprised at the thickness of his body. Joe Frazier and Mike Tyson were short heavyweights, but had very thick, muscular bodies. In person, "Big" George Foreman looked as huge and round as a big oak tree. Foreman was big even by pro football standards. McKnight was taller than most heavyweights – even Foreman and Ali – but he didn't possess a thick torso.

Despite the critics, McKnight amassed a very impressive pro record of 33 wins and only one defeat, and 22 of his triumphs were by knockout. He was so quick and elusive that Foreman, the former heavyweight champion, refused to fight him.

Foreman's promoter, Bob Arum of Top Rank Inc., had a fight for Foreman on cable television giant HBO. Sean Gibbons, one of Top Rank's matchmakers, called me in 1997 and said, "We've got an HBO date for Big George in April. I need you to send some video of McKnight's fights for Foreman to look at. We might be able to get your guy a date on HBO with the champ."

Obviously, we were quite excited about this potential opportunity because a win against the legendary, former two-time world champion would put McKnight in the driver's seat. Boxers dream of these opportunities. A fight on HBO against Foreman could have paid McKnight more than $200,000. I hurriedly put some highlights together and sent the video the next day. After Foreman reviewed the tape, he turned McKnight down as his opponent. Instead, Foreman chose the stronger, less mobile Lou Savarese as his opponent instead of McKnight. While on a speaking engagement in Nashville, Foreman told *Nashville Banner* sportswriter Randy Weiler that he didn't want to face the skillful McKnight because he was too quick and elusive.

"I don't want to fight somebody I've got to chase around that ring," Foreman said. "Somebody's gonna get their jaw hurt fighting that boy."

In addition to being a great champion, Foreman had a wonderful sense of humor. When asked once whether he worried about brain damage, he said, "Not really. Anybody going into boxing already has brain damage." Maybe there is some truth to that statement, but George Foreman was one of the shrewdest businessmen in the history of the sport.

Heavyweight Keith McKnight towers above a fallen opponent.

McKnight's Greatest Triumph

Keith McKnight never won a world title, never fought for a world title and never had a million-dollar payday. But, he still was a success in the sport of boxing. I was never prouder of him than the night he faced and defeated the dangerous Phil Jackson, a former challenger for the world heavyweight title. To this day, I am proud of how I helped move McKnight into a position to fight fighters of Jackson's caliber.

Team McKnight had signed an agreement with one of boxing's premier promoters, Cedric Kushner, a year before the potential Foreman bout. Kushner put McKnight in four televised bouts. McKnight won all four bouts and was on a roll. In the first of the four fights, McKnight knocked out rugged, power-punching Tui Toia of Samoa in the first round of their bout in Houston in July 1996. In his next TV fight, McKnight scored a 10-round unanimous decision against tough Eddie Donaldson in Asbury Park, N.J., in May 1997. Then, McKnight registered a quick, first-round knockout of big Brian Scott in a match at the Nez Perce Indian Reservation in Lewiston, Idaho, in July. The biggest fight of McKnight's career, against Jackson in Nashville, came next.

The day McKnight faced Jackson was one of the hardest days of my life. While training for the Jackson bout, Diane, my precious wife of 28 years, was diagnosed with breast cancer. She had a mastectomy just a few days before the bout, and we brought her home from the hospital on Oct. 2, 1997, the day of the McKnight-Jackson fight.

Diane's mother came to stay with us to help take care of her for a few days. Even though she wasn't in imminent danger, I wanted to stay home with her that night, but she insisted that I be with Keith. She had watched him grow up, and had come to love him. She was more concerned about his welfare than her own.

Fortunately, Municipal Auditorium, the fight venue, was only 30 minutes from our home. Rev. Ken Collins, my close friend, rode with me to the fight, and tried to minister to me along the way. But I was in agony because of my wife's illness. The stress almost was unbearable. I had a hard time functioning that night; in addition to worrying about my wife, I was concerned about the danger McKnight might face that evening from the power-punching Jackson.

When we entered the dressing room, I wrapped Keith's hands using two rolls of gauze for each hand, as was our custom. McKnight began warming up for the bout by shadow boxing. After he broke a sweat, we put Vaseline on his face and body to protect him against getting cut. He put on his large leather protective cup and boxing trunks. Then we put the 10-ounce Mexican-manufactured Reyes boxing gloves on him. In my opinion, they are the world's finest boxing glove. They are called a puncher's glove because they conform so tightly to a boxer's fist. When you hit someone with a Reyes glove on, it's almost like hitting them with your bare knuckles. This would benefit Jackson, our opponent, because he was a purebred, bona-fide puncher. It was nearly time to start our walk to the ring.

We sat in the dressing room and waited on the call for the main event fighters to start toward the ring. In the other dressing room, McKnight's dangerous opponent also was preparing.

Phil Jackson had fought Lennox Lewis for the heavyweight world championship. Jackson was no joke as a fighter. He was a bad dude who was on a mission in the ring, and if you were in the other corner, he intended to hurt you. Many boxing people referred to Jackson as a killer. He hit with astounding power. He was a one-punch knockout artist, and he could knock you out with either hand and, just like former heavyweight champion Mike Tyson, he came after you with bad intentions.

Fight The Good Fight

During the second round of the fight, Jackson walked to the center of the ring and, with precision timing, threw a devastating right hand that caught McKnight squarely on the chin and sent him crashing to the canvas. Most fighters would have lain down and let the referee count them out after being brutalized by such tremendous power. A fighter with no courage would surely melt like wax after being hit by one of the hardest punchers in the world. They would take the easy way out and not get up. However, after being knocked down, McKnight rolled over and stabilized himself on one knee.

When the referee's count reached eight, McKnight rose to his feet and tried to shake the cobwebs from his head. After the referee wiped McKnight's gloves off, he moved out of the way and motioned the fighters to continue boxing. Jackson, like a lion after his prey, swarmed McKnight. Jackson faked a jab and threw another crushing right hand that landed flush on McKnight's jaw, sending him to the canvas once again.

A smart fighter doesn't jump right up after being knocked down because he is still groggy. Physically, he's like a person who has had too much to drink. He is under the influence, but it's not liquor that's making him unsteady. A boxer who stands up too soon might stumble and cause the referee to stop the fight. As McKnight rolled over and raised his body up on one knee for the second time in less than a minute, awaiting the referee's eight-count, he threw a frustrated look at me in our corner.

In desperation, I hollered to him, "You've got to take it to him. You've got to fight him."

When the referee allowed the bout to continue, hundreds of hometown McKnight fans started hollering and encouraging him. Keith went straight at Jackson and pushed him across the ring; the fighters then went into a clinch. McKnight wisely used this opportunity to tie Jackson up long enough to clear his head and to allow the bell to ring, ending the round.

Mark Frazee had been a world-class middleweight boxer during his career, but was now retired. He had helped train McKnight for this bout and he was assisting me in the corner, so we did our best to calm McKnight. It was only the second round. We didn't want Keith to panic and reassured him that he had plenty of time to win the bout. We took sponges of cold water and squeezed them over his head, neck and body. We washed out his mouthpiece, massaged his body and gave him water to drink.

When the bell sounded to begin the third round, the fans in attendance began to chant "Keith, Keith, Keith, Keith. ..." This energized McKnight, and he soon got into a smooth boxing rhythm. He began moving around the ring like a master matador, hitting Jackson with that pretty left jab of his pop, pop, pop! Pop, pop, pop!

As the rounds progressed, McKnight also began to catch Jackson with nice combinations. He would throw four or five quick punches in succession – bing, bing, bing bing! Bing, bing! Boom! McKnight was starting to sting and frustrate Jackson. In desperation, Jackson tried to catch McKnight with wild, thunderous punches – attempting to knock him out.

McKnight was younger, faster and more mobile than Jackson, and he eluded Jackson's big bombs and then nailed Jackson with counter punches. Every time Jackson loaded up and threw one of those bombs, McKnight slipped away to avoid getting hit and returned fire, catching the angry, frustrated Jackson clean. As the fight wore on, McKnight took control and was winning the bout with his smooth, graceful boxing skills. Between the ninth and 10th rounds, Jackson walked back to his corner and sat down on his stool. His Cuban trainer slapped him in the face and started screaming at him, telling him he was losing the fight. He shouted, "You've got to knock him out to win!"

In the 10th round, Jackson came out looking to end the fight with one of those big power shots. McKnight was boxing in a graceful rhythm and was catching Jackson with fast, clean, shots as he maneuvered out of the way without getting hit. The bell rang, ending the bout. The judges tabulated their scorecards – and McKnight had won a unanimous decision against the most dangerous fighter he had ever faced. For the critics who said that McKnight had beaten a faded fighter, Jackson went on to knock out his next six consecutive opponents. I was so proud of Keith in his victory against Jackson. It was a very tough, hard fight, but he had prevailed. I thought that this win would give McKnight the confidence to beat anyone in the world.

Boxing trainer Luther Burgess told me a story about the young Cassius Clay before he became Muhammad Ali. He said before Clay had beaten Sonny Liston he really didn't believe he could beat everyone in the heavyweight division. However, after he had beaten Liston this gave him the confidence that he was truly the best heavyweight in the world. Jackson and Liston both were deadly punchers. I thought that this huge victory would help Keith overcome some of his doubts about his own ability. Against top-level fighters, he had a tendency to fight hesitantly and I was hopeful that this would give him the confidence he needed to take the initiative to fight more aggressively against better competition since he had a propensity to freeze in big bouts.

During World War II when Great Britain faced Nazi Germany, British Prime Minister Sir Winston Churchill said, "Never, never, never, never, never give up." Great Britain didn't give up, and it eventually prevailed against Nazi Germany's onslaught and their evil leader Adolph Hitler. .

McKnight epitomized Churchill's words when he picked himself up off of the floor not once, but twice to beat the

Fight The Good Fight

hazardous Phil Jackson. That night was McKnight's finest hour as a professional boxer; he wouldn't give up.

To this day, I remain proud of Keith McKnight for overcoming his doubts, not giving up and defeating a fighter the caliber of Phil Jackson.

Dueling Head Butts

On May 5, 1992, my boxer, Tim "Scrap Iron" Johnson, was fighting David Bates, a rugged, awkward boxer from Odessa, Texas, in the main event of a boxing show, at the New Daisy Theatre on Beale Street in Memphis, Tennessee. Bates accidentally had struck Johnson with a head butt. Johnson was steaming mad when he sat down on his stool in our corner between rounds.

"Kerry, he just hit me with a head butt," Johnson said.

"It was probably an accident, but be careful and don't get cut," I replied.

"I'm going to get him back." Johnson responded.

As the bell sounded for the next round to begin, Johnson rushed across the ring and like a battering ram smashed his head into Bates' forehead, opening a huge gash on Johnson's own head. After the show that evening, Johnson and I spent the rest of the night in a hospital emergency room having staples put into his skull to close the wound he had inflicted on himself.

Such was the life and times of Timmy Johnson. His parents had deserted Timmy in a laundromat as a child. He ended up in The Tennessee Baptist Children's home as an orphan. When he was 13, Tommy and Pat Johnson, adopted him. They were a wonderful Christian couple who had three children of their own to raise but had given their lives to the care and nurturing of other children as well. Timmy was their first adopted child and he took on the family name.

I began teaching Johnson how to box when he was 18 years old. He was a very handsome young man with great charisma. I remember a time while we were eating dinner the night before he was to compete as an amateur boxer in the Southern Golden Gloves tournament in Knoxville, Tennessee. A waitress walked over to our table and asked him,

Fight The Good Fight

"Do you have a girlfriend?" and before he had time to reply she said, "Would you like one?"

I knew that he had a rough time growing up before meeting his adoptive parents. I could see from the way he acted that there had been some trauma in his life. He could be the nicest person in the world one minute, and then something would set him off and he would erupt into a rage. Although I was constantly in a battle with him, I grew to love the kid and the family as well. He reminded me so much of myself when I was younger. He was wounded, angry, bitter, and carrying a chip on his shoulder just like I had been for many years of my life. He could also pass as my own cousin Timmy Pharr's twin.

Johnson was a tough guy, cocky and a brawler. He was such a scrapper that we nicknamed him "Scrap Iron." We also referred to him as T.J. He liked the verbal confrontations as much as the physical ones. He emulated Muhammad Ali and engaged in trash talking with his opponent and others who wanted to join in on the verbal sparring.

'Geez, Timmy, I Didn't Mean For You to Kill Him'

T.J. wasn't a tremendous puncher, but I remember an incident while he was an amateur where he hurt another boxer and it was my fault. Our original boxing team was named Club Knockout by a local newspaper reporter. The guys liked the moniker and it was our team name for 10 years. Johnson, Ken "The Bull" Atkin and "Dangerous" Don Wilford were the original three team members of Club Knockout. I began training Atkin and Jeff Bowman of Nashville a couple of years earlier on a team sponsored by Universal Health Spa, a business that Jeff's father, Randall, and I owned at the time.

Our young team was training in a baseball announcer's building that the mayor of La Vergne, Tennessee, allowed us to use as a gym. It was a small cinderblock building with a carpeted wooden floor upstairs that we roped off and used as a boxing ring. We had about 20 young men who were learning how to box in the building.

A tall, rugged fellow by the name of Lonnie was training with us. Lonnie was about 21. He didn't follow instructions well. In fact, he wouldn't do anything I asked him to do. Each time I let him spar he tried to murder his sparring partner. In the gym I never allowed one boxer to abuse another. Since the guys were boxing and hitting each other, obviously someone would get clipped on the chin and would get knocked down or knocked out. But that was a rare occasion. The boxers always wore protective gear, and we were careful not to let things get out of control in practice. They would spar in 16-ounce training gloves and wear a headgear, a protective cup and a mouthpiece.

I was a relatively young coach and didn't handle the following situation very well. I was trying to teach Lonnie and the other fellows how to box. I normally worked with a boxer for several weeks on technique on the heavy-bag, double end bag and speed bag before I would allow them to begin "controlled sparring." We would put sparring gloves on two boxers of the same age, weight and skill level and I would allow them to spar with each other using only the jab.

The jab is the most important punch a boxer learns. It isn't the most powerful punch, but it is usually the most effective punch. A boxer always leads with a jab. It sets all the other punches up. Former world heavyweight champion Larry Holmes dominated the division for seven years, largely on the strength of his great left jab. Holmes realized that to control an opponent in a match, you have to establish the jab first. For a right-handed boxer, the left jab is the lead but the right hand, the left hook and the uppercut are the power punches. The jab is the first punch that you teach to a new boxer. The other punches take months and even years to learn and to incorporate into your fistic arsenal.

Lonnie was sparring with another boxer and the other youngster, as instructed, was using only his jab. Even though I had asked Lonnie to use only his left jab, Lonnie threw wild right hands and screamed at his sparring partners, intentionally trying to hurt them. I was frustrated and angry with him, and I could see that I was going to have to put someone else with experience in to spar with Lonnie.

Tim Johnson, Ken Atkin and Don Wilford had been training for a couple of months more than Lonnie. So I gloved Johnson up, who was 19, and whispered in his ear, "I want you to teach this kid a lesson."

Both of the boxers were gloved and ready to spar. When the bell rang to begin the round, Lonnie let out a blood-curdling scream and charged across the ring toward Johnson. I believe that it actually scared Timmy, and out of fear he threw an incredibly vicious wild right hand that landed squarely on Lonnie's mouth.

Lonnie crashed to the floor, and the building shook like we were in an earthquake. Johnson knocked Lonnie out cold; he was bleeding from the mouth where the punch had caused a tooth to puncture his lip. His face was as white as a ghost and he looked seriously hurt. It was a very scary moment for me and I turned to Johnson and said, "Gees Timmy, I didn't mean for you to kill him!"

Jimmy Brindley, another boxer, was standing by watching the sparring. Seeing Lonnie get knocked out so viciously scared Brindley so much that he immediately took off his gloves, left the boxing gym and never returned.

He later told another boxer, "Man, he hit him so hard I saw the light. That's the end of my boxing career."

About 15 or 20 seconds later Lonnie came to. He needed a few stitches in his mouth, but other than his pride being hurt he was OK. I don't know why, but he never returned to the boxing gym, either.

As an amateur, Johnson won the Mid-State Golden Gloves and several other regional tournaments. Early on in his professional boxing career he had some really great opportunities. In fact, he fought for two world championships.

He faced the hard-hitting Randall Younker on June 15, 1992, for the World Boxing Federation light-heavyweight world championship just five weeks after the bout with Bates, and was stopped in the fifth round. Johnson was much more competitive in the lighter super-middleweight division.

Johnson and I traveled to Brazil in November of 1993 where Johnson was to face Luciana Torres for the WBF super-middleweight world championship a day before Thanksgiving. This was a bout that Johnson could have won, had he not suffered a cut from a clash of heads with Torres. While in Brazil the promoter, as is customary in most promotions, took us around the large city of Recife for newspaper, radio and television appearances to help promote the upcoming championship fight.

Fight The Good Fight

While we were in a large open-air market, Johnson and some of the local Brazilian vendors started trading insults. Johnson said something that offended the local butcher, and he came from behind his counter and began to threaten us with a machete in front of a large crowd of excited Brazilians. Johnson wisely toned down the rhetoric and we escaped without injury.

Although it was November and the weather in the states was colder, we were south of the equator and it was the opposite in Brazil. The fight was held in an open-air arena and it was very hot and steamy in the packed auditorium that night.

Johnson was boxing really well against the Brazilian they called "Todo Duro" which translated means "Hard as Steel." Johnson had been cut in the second or third round of the fight but was out-boxing Torres in spite of the cut. During the bout, Johnson would stop and taunt Torres. This sent the partisan crowd into frenzy. They became so enraged with Johnson's antics that they began to throw things into the ring. This only added fuel to the fire for Johnson, who was getting attention for his showboating. He grew braver as the fight progressed.

Torres never hurt Johnson and the cut wasn't that serious; however, during the eighth round, the referee stepped in and stopped the fight. Johnson was extremely disappointed because he thought he was close to winning a world championship. The crowd who had been so furious with Johnson during the fight embraced him afterward and mobbed him like he was a rock star. For Johnson who had seen so little love as a child this adulation was overwhelming. He was starving for affection, but he couldn't absorb enough from this loving crowd to heal the deep-rooted pain he had suffered as a child.

Chapter 4: Women of Steel

Angie

I first met Angie when she was 18. She was very pretty, with blue eyes and long golden hair. She was married to a handsome young man. They were a great-looking young couple that reminded people of Ken and Barbie. Angie and her husband were in the ministry together. They sang duets, and Angie was a ventriloquist who ministered to children with her sidekick "Danny the Dummy."

Her husband wanted to start a home for troubled teenage boys. He and Angie took several young men into their home to minister to them. The young married couple seemed perfect for one another. They appeared very happy and deeply in love with each other. Angie's hair was very long and I remember a young teenage boy asking her if she wanted to cut her hair.

Her protective husband responded with a strong no. "I like her just the way she is."

After overhearing that conversation, I believed that he was an adoring husband. However, there was a dark side to her handsome young husband that none of us knew about. Later Angie learned that her husband was consumed by homosexuality. She met with our pastor for counseling. He advised her to separate from her husband to give him time to repent of his sinful lifestyle and change his ways. Angie stayed by his side for another year as she tried to help him overcome his wayward lifestyle.

Instead of repenting, he sank deeper and deeper into his obsession, contracted AIDS and consequently died from this dreaded disease.

Angie became a widow at a very young age. She had also lost her mother and her grandparents before she married. However, her faith in Christ was strong and she didn't waver in her service to the Lord. She continued serving the Lord and living an exemplary life, trusting him completely even after experiencing so much tragedy.

Several years later, Angie began dating a man from church named Fred. Fred had lost his wife to cancer and was rearing two children on his own. Angie fell in love with Fred and they married. She became a great mother for Fred's children and loved them as deeply as her own. She and Fred had a son and named him Jonathon. Angie also became my wife Diane's dearest friend.

Years after Jonathon's birth, Angie learned that she had leukemia. She met with her doctors and they gave her a grim statistical viewpoint of her prognosis. However, Angie said that she wasn't a statistic, but a child of the living God. She never became discouraged and never lacked hope. She believed that God, in His infinite mercy, would heal her sick body. Like the Eveready bunny she just kept going, going and going. She was an unbelievable inspiration to everyone around her. About a week before her fifth-year anniversary of being cancer free, Angie had a relapse. This was enough to knock a normal person to the ground. But Angie wasn't normal, and when she received the bad report she just placed her eyes and faith on Jesus and continued to believe that she would be completely healed.

Fight The Good Fight

Several years later her husband Fred, a manic depressant, quit taking his medication. He lost his job and began to sink deeper and deeper into hopelessness. One day he didn't come home. It seemed like he had just disappeared. His parked car was found south of Nashville, Tennessee, on the Natchez Trace Parkway. There were no signs of foul play and nothing was out of order in his vehicle. Numerous search parties combed the wooded area where his car was found but discovered nothing. Several months later, another search party that included his daughter Julie searched the wooded area again. This time they discovered Fred's body. Sadly, in his weakened mental state he had committed suicide.

Angie and the children were devastated. Angie pressed on, her faith never wavering. Today she is still living a victorious Christian life while continuing to raise her and Fred's teenage son Jonathon.

Aunt Reubene

Aunt Reubene was married to my dad's older brother W.B. My Dad and W.B. got into all sorts of interesting scrapes in their early years. W.B. struggled with the bottle for much of his adult life. Perhaps the best thing W.B. ever did was marrying Reubene Stacy, a lovely Christian young lady who lived in the community. Reubene is a dear Christian woman who struggled with my uncle's lifestyle for many years in much the same way my mother did with my father. Obviously she didn't realize how the bottle would take control of his life.

W.B. and Reubene found work at American Motors, an auto factory in Wisconsin, and like so many poor southern farmers moved their family there for a better life.

While living in an area where there was a tavern on almost every block, W.B. began to drink more and more. Soon he could no longer control it and he became an alcoholic.

I was about 11, and remember being afraid of him. On one particular occasion he scared me so much that I climbed a tree to get away from him while he was drunk.

He was really hard on Reubene and the boys. Reubene put up with his drinking for years. Then finally, he lost his job at American Motors because of his drinking. He became worse and worse, until Reubene asked him to move out of their home. He moved out and sank deeper into alcoholism. Finally, Aunt Reubene and a couple of other family members signed a petition and had him committed to an alcohol rehabilitation center. He went through the treatment program until he was strong enough to refuse liquor placed in front of him.

He was released and never drank again for the rest of his life. Unfortunately, he had liver disease from the excessive amounts of alcohol, and emphysema from a lifelong habit of smoking Camel cigarettes. Reubene took him back, and he also got his job back at American Motors and lived a productive life. During the next 10 or 12 years, we had a lot of fun together. W.B. always was willing to help those he loved, and was quick to be there to loan money or co-sign a note for a family member who needed help. He even protected me when I was in trouble and running from the law. When threatened with jail time by the authorities, they asked him why he helped me. He simply replied, "He's my nephew."

He wouldn't betray a friend or family member for any amount of money.

His health continually declined and we lost W.B. at age 55. I sure miss him.

W.B. and Reubene's boys were my cousins Phillip, Charles and Timmy. Phillip and I were about the same age so we were constant companions in our teenage years. Charles and Timmy were a few years younger, and they experimented with drugs; Timmy became hooked on them at a very young age.

Timmy overdosed on drugs on several different occasions. I remember standing by his hospital bed after an overdose when he was just 16 years old, not knowing if he would survive until the next morning. He survived that overdose and several others.

I loved him dearly and I wanted to help him overcome this addiction. I asked him to come and stay with my wife, daughter and me for a while. My aunt and uncle agreed, so he stayed at our house for a couple of months that year, later moving back home with his parents.

Timmy had another scare a couple of years later with a drug overdose. He went through the Teen Challenge drug rehabilitation program in Chicago. David Wilkerson had founded Teen Challenge, which is a Biblically based drug and alcohol recovery program. While there, Timmy prayed and asked Christ to come into his heart but he became addicted to drugs while he was so young that he struggled almost every day of his life with the demons of drug addiction. He tried heroin at a very young age and many other hard drugs before he was even old enough to drive.

He'd been in jail and prison on numerous occasions because of the drugs. He had lived a hard, fast life and was now in his late 30s. He temporarily had cleaned up his life and was going to church, reading his Bible and praying every day. His mother Reubene told me she would hear him in his bedroom at night crying out to the Lord to help him overcome his cravings for drugs.

Timmy called me on a Monday and we had a great conversation about the Lord. He told me that Aunt Reubene was taking him to work every day and that they prayed together before he got out of the car.

Later that same week something happened to depress him and he decided to purchase some heroin. He and his grown son Shawn, whom he had fathered when he was 13, purchased a significant amount of heroin. Timmy and Shawn went to a friend's house where they both injected a shot of heroin into their veins. Shawn and the friend decided to leave the house to buy some hamburgers and fries. Timmy was alone at the house with the rest of the heroin in his possession. While Shawn and the friend were away, Timmy injected another large dose of heroin into his veins, which instantly stopped his heart. When Shawn and the friend returned they found Timmy's lifeless body on the bed. This last shot of heroin took his life.

He had named Christ as his savior, but the drug addiction controlled him and took his life at a young age.

I took Timmy to the boxing gym when he was 13 and he trained for a couple of months. He looked really good in sparring sessions against older experienced boxers. I'm certain he would have been a good fighter had he stayed with it. In my experience as a trainer I've witnessed several young men battle drug problems while attempting to box.

Fight The Good Fight

They didn't do drugs while in the gym but I knew who most of them were. It was rare to see any of them give up their habit for the sport. Once you start down that road it is so hard to put it down.

Sadly, some time later Reubene also lost her middle son Charles to liver cancer. Earlier in his life Charles had also used drugs intravenously and had contracted hepatitis. This eventually became cancer and took his life at a very young age. Fortunately God in his mercy allowed Charles to live long enough to give his life to Christ before he passed away.

Through all of these trials and tribulations with her husband and children, Reubene remained faithful to her wedding vows, her husband, her children and her Lord and Savior Jesus Christ. She never dated or remarried. She is an amazing Christian woman. For the Christian, there is no pain in this life that heaven will not heal. The Christian will only see pain and sorrow in this life. In heaven they will see only joy, happiness and perfect contentment. However, the unbeliever will only see a glimpse of goodness in this life. Once he passes the portals of death, he will experience nothing but sorrow and pain.

Lanita

Several months after my first wife Diane passed away, I was at a Christian organization's Valentine's Day party. After dinner, three ladies walked to the table I was sharing with a group of others. The blonde with the pretty green eyes immediately caught my attention. She looked too young for me, but she asked if anyone was sitting in the chair next to me. I responded with a quick, "You are."

She laughed as she and her two friends took a seat at our table. As the night progressed, I learned that although she looked much younger than her age, she was only five years younger than me. I told her I had lost my wife to breast cancer several months earlier. She then told me about losing her husband Steve in a boating accident some 20 years earlier. She was left a widow with four young children to raise on her own. I also learned that she had lost her first-born son Steven when he was only four days old. After her husband Steve passed away, she had a very difficult time emotionally and went to counseling to deal with her grief. But there was little time to mourn, as she had to take care of her four children. One of her children, Jayna, was born with severe digestive problems. Her stomach, intestines and bladder didn't function, and most children with this disease died from malnutrition or infection. Lanita was her caregiver for the next year and a half until little 2-year-old Jayna died and went home to be with the Lord. This was such a heavy burden for Lanita, who was trying to hold her young family together.

She pressed on for the next five or six years alone, until she met a man and fell in love. She mistakenly married this person who ended up being mean to her and her children. She tried to make the marriage work, but the circumstances grew worse during the next 10 years. He became both verbally and physically abusive. Her husband wrapped his hands

Fight The Good Fight

around her teenage son's throat and tried to choke him. The husband started staying away from the home for weeks at a time, pretty much deserting Lanita emotionally. Lanita tried to make their marriage work, and even asked her husband to go to counseling with her. When she saw there was no hope for the marriage, she filed for divorce.

One of Lanita's three surviving children had a hard time dealing with her father's death and subsequent stepfather's abuse, and is battling alcoholism and drug addiction today.

Through all of this pain and heartache Lanita has continued to go to church and has maintained her faith and walk with the Lord.

As I write these words, Lanita and I have been married for more than four years. She is still very pretty, a great friend and a wonderful wife, who is full of joy and loves to laugh. We both lost our childhood sweethearts to an untimely death. But we are thankful to the Lord for each other.

Maybe you have gone through a tragic time in your life. Maybe you think there will never be a brighter day. Don't despair; there can be joy, peace and happiness in your life again.

"To everything there is a season, a time for every purpose under heaven: A time to weep, and a time to laugh; a time to mourn, and a time to dance." Ecclesiastes 3:1 and 4.

Rita

While my wife Diane was Pastor Al Henson's secretary at Lighthouse Baptist Church in Antioch, Tennessee, in the early 1980s, we met Rita Doyle. She was a charming woman who was also on staff at the church. She was the executive assistant to Lee Jennings, the administrator of the ministries at that time. Rita is an amazing and interesting lady. She is bright, energetic, determined, humorous and also very independent. She and Diane became very close while working together.

Rita announced one day to the pastoral staff that she felt that the Lord was leading her to become a missionary to South Korea. Knowing how difficult it would be for a young woman on the mission field, the men on staff at Lighthouse basically said to Rita, "Are you insane?"

Rita felt this calling very strongly and wasn't about to be discouraged from doing what she believed the Lord was leading her to do. During the next couple of years, she started preparing for the work the Lord had called her to do. She began by learning the language. She spoke to churches and individuals to raise the support she needed to carry out the work. It was very difficult but, eventually she raised the support. With the help of Pioneer Mission Board, she moved by herself to Seoul, South Korea, as a missionary.

She served there for a couple of years and then encountered health problems. Rita had kidney stones and went into a hospital. The kidney stones needed to be removed, but the surgeon didn't take them out. After she was released, one of her kidneys became infected; she became very ill and almost died while there. She returned to Nashville for medical tests and learned that her kidney was destroyed. She was operated on to have the lifeless kidney removed. Diane stayed by her side in the hospital as they prepared her for surgery and spent a great deal of time ministering to her afterward.

Rita spent several months recuperating from the surgery and then returned to Korea. She was there for five years and felt she would be of more use ministering elsewhere. So she returned to the United States and prayed about where the Lord would send her next. After much prayerful consideration, she told everyone she thought the Lord was calling her back to the mission field.

"Where do you think he wants you to go?" she was asked. "I think He wants me to go minister to the Reindeer people in Mongolia," she would say. Everyone was shocked and really believed she was insane this time. These people live in one of the most barren, frigid, remote mountainous places on Earth. Many folks tried to discourage her from going to such a dangerous place described as Outer Mongolia. But Rita wouldn't be denied as she began learning another foreign language and started raising support so she would be able to take the Gospel of Jesus Christ to these isolated people far away on a desolate corner of the globe.

Rita again learned a new language, raised support and went to live in Mongolia. She was alone and seemingly defenseless in a strange country. She settled in Tsaagan Nuur and started teaching the poor people there about Jesus Christ. It was a very dangerous land where the Mongol men often got drunk and were notorious for coming home and beating their wives and children. Often the women would send their children to spend the night with Rita until their husbands sobered up. One night, Rita was caught in a building hallway when one of the drunken Mongolian men grabbed her and tried to assault her. Rita was able to fend off her attacker long enough to escape and reach safety.

While there, she lived in a hut the Mongols called "a ger." It is similar to a round tent with a door in the front of it Many times the drunken men would come to her house late in the night and try to break down her door. One night a man started pounding on her door and broke it off of the hinges.

Rita was on one side of the door pushing against the man who was on the other side pushing against her trying to get in. Suddenly, he gave up and walked away. Rita believes it was the Lord who intervened and kept her from being harmed since the door was completely loose and suspended between the two of them. Through all of this she stayed in Mongolia for 13 years teaching the locals the Gospel of Jesus Christ.

When my wife Diane was diagnosed with breast cancer and was lying on a gurney in the hospital about to be wheeled into the operating room for a mastectomy, a nurse approached us just as they were rolling Diane away for her operation. The nurse told Diane, "I have something for you." She handed me a bouquet of flowers and presented the card to Diane. When she opened the card, she read, "You were there for me. I'm sorry I can't be there with you. I love you and I'm praying for you. Rita Doyle." When Diane realized Rita had arranged to send those flowers from Mongolia, she began to cry knowing the love Rita had expressed toward her. It was one of the most touching moments of my life.

The living conditions are deplorable in Mongolia and many orphan babies die because of the lack of care in the orphanages. This burdened the tender hearted Rita and while visiting an orphanage she saw a beautiful little Mongolian baby near death. Rita was heartbroken over the child and started making arrangements to adopt the tiny infant. She was able to adopt the child and once she got her out of the orphanage she took her to a Doctor where she was able to get the child she named Kaitlyn temporary medical care.

Kaitlyn had medical problems and a learning disability. Rita began to realize how dangerous it was becoming for her and Kaitlyn to be in Mongolia. She also understood that Kaitlyn could receive better medical care in the United States so she made arrangements to get Kaitlyn and her out of Mongolia. Once they arrived in the United States, Rita

Fight The Good Fight

was able to get little Kaitlyn great medical care, but it took several years of good health care to get the child healthy.

After Rita returned to the United States, she was sponsored by a Phoenix church to minister to the Native Americans in Arizona. Some time later, the church pastor resigned and Rita lost her support. She now is working a job in Phoenix and continues her ministry to Native American women in the Phoenix area. Little Kaitlyn, 7, attends school. Rita said she feels the Lord wants her to start a foster home to care and minister to orphaned children. Please don't tell her she can't do it. If you feel led to help fund her work, here is the mission board's address:

Rita Doyle/Missionary
Attention: Ms. Hutton
Colorado Missionary Society
6057 W. Ottawa Ave. Suite C7
Littleton, CO 80128

Chapter 5: Life lessons

Learning to Heal

Healing for me was slow in coming, but it did come. God gave me another wonderful Christian wife, Lanita, who also had experienced the pain of losing loved ones so dear. She had experienced the death of her father, her husband and two of her young children. Life still has many challenges for Lanita and me, but is enjoyable for us again.

> *"My brethren, count it all joy when you fall into various trials, knowing that the testing of your faith produces patience."* (James 1:2)

All of us are going to face various trials in this world and in life. But don't give up and don't give in. These trials actually produce character for those who follow Jesus Christ. After the darkness of night, the morning always brings sunlight. Remember, there will be a brighter day. Have faith in God and don't quit. I have found strength in the words of the following poem:

Fight The Good Fight

When things go wrong as they sometimes will.
When the road you're trudging seems all up hill.
When funds are low and the debts are high.
And you want to smile, but you have to sigh.
When care is pressing you down a bit.
Rest, if you must, but don't you quit.
Life is queer with its twists and turns.
As everyone of us sometimes learns.
And many a failure turns about.
When he might have won had he stuck it out:
Don't give up though the pace seems slow –
You may succeed with another blow.
Success is failure turned inside out –
The silver tint of the clouds of doubt
And you never can tell how close you are.
It may be near when it seems so far:
So stick to the fight when you're hardest hit –
It's when things seem worst that you must not quit.

Author Unknown

Life Is Stressful

We live such a fast-paced life these days. Every time we go shopping at a store or to the mall, it seems we have to stand in an endless line for service. Driving to work is an incredible challenge in most cities today. You face what seems like an endless array of red lights or have to sit indefinitely in rush-hour traffic. Our patience is tested daily. Our blood pressure increases, causing an unhealthy situation.

If you don't move quickly while sitting at a red light that just turned green, those behind you will began to blow their horn at you, curse you and make obscene gestures toward you. We live in an angry, sinful world where many people do not show common courtesy for their fellow man. Many of us are stressed and usually are looking to vent our anger and frustration on someone.

I know a person in Dallas who had the misfortune of being in a highway lane for a moment too long, preventing a carload of young thugs from passing him immediately. They became angered; someone in the vehicle pulled a gun and began shooting. My friend was in a van and he began to drive in a defensive manner so as to not get hit by the bullets. He said later he did not want to leave his two children as orphans. Fortunately, he escaped without being hit by the bullets.

Damaged Goods

In professional boxing, a fighter who has fought for many years and has taken a lot of punishment is considered "damaged goods." Those who have suffered abuse as a child or have unresolved trauma are the ones who are really damaged goods. Psychologists tell us that abuse as a child leads to alcohol, drug, food and sexual addictions. It also causes many people to carry extreme anger, hatred and violence into adulthood. Many of these people are walking time bombs waiting to explode.

As a boxing coach and as a businessman, I ran a gym and owned a health club for many years. Obviously, when you get a group of young men together there will be a certain amount of fun, horseplay and tricks played on one another. Most of the time, it was a barrel of laughs, but on several occasions someone would get angry and a fight would ensue.

There was a parent of one of our boxers who had never boxed, but was a big, burly man. He was also a little bit of a bully. The parent, who was in his 40s at the time, came into the gym one day and wrestled one of the professional boxers to the floor. The person he wrestled to the floor was a good-natured guy, and he didn't get very upset. In fact, everyone got a chuckle out of the incident.

The next day the parent returned and decided he would repeat the horseplay. However, on this day, he picked on a good amateur boxer who was loaded with anger and a bad attitude. When the parent wrestled this 20-year-old boxer to the ground, he stepped on the boxer's finger, which infuriated the fighter. The boxer exploded with anger, jumped up and punched the bullying parent, busting his lip and "knocking the daylights" out of him.

"I'll kill you, boy," the enraged parent screamed as he grabbed a metal chair as a weapon and chased the boxer around the ring.

Ken Atkin and I were trying to take the chair away from the furious parent, who suddenly ran out of the gym to his truck to get a weapon. Finally, everyone cooled down and the angry parent felt bad about his behavior. However, he could have killed the young man in a moment of rage if he had had a gun or a knife in his hand.

"Dangerous" Don Wilford is the nicest gentleman you will ever meet. Wilford began boxing at age 26 and fought as an amateur for two years, turning professional at 28. His professional record was 21-3. He had blazing hand speed and good punching power. If he had started boxing as a teenager, he would have become a world champion. But he began his career so late in life that he didn't have enough time to develop his skills. The gifted Wilford fought as a welterweight at 147 pounds.

James "J.R." Spears, another boxer who trained with Don, also is a great guy. Spears won a national light-heavy-weight amateur championship before he became a professional boxer. Spears has a heart of gold, but he loves talking trash. He fought as a light-heavyweight at 178 pounds. He would find someone in the gym to pick on, and every day when that person arrived at the gym Spears would light into them and start verbally abusing them.

Spears absolutely was harmless, but there's no way of knowing how many new boxers he ran off with his demeanor and his mouth. When a new boxer would walk into the gym, Spears would holler, "Fresh meat. That's my meat."

It scared some new boxers and angered others. For about a month, Spears harassed Wilford every day when he arrived at the gym. He got in Don's face and started belittling him and asking him, "How come you're late? Are you scared of me? You don't want none of me do you? I own you! I'm your daddy," and any other thing he could think of to intimidate Don.

On one particular day, Spears and Wilford were sparring when the bell rang to end the first round. Don walked to his corner and I held out a water bottle for him to take a drink. Spears started berating Don again. Something was troubling Don that day. He had had enough of J.R.'s mouth. Don walked from his corner across the ring to the corner where Spears was standing and threw a furious right hand that landed flush on Spears jaw.

Spears, who had a granite chin, was one of the toughest guys I have ever seen. He just blinked his eyes and rolled his head after being clobbered by Wilford. I rushed into the ring thinking I was going to have to separate these two.

Spears looked at me and said, "That's all right I'll get mine when the bell rings."

When the bell rang, Spears went after Wilford like a man possessed, but Wilford was just too quick for the 40-plus-year-old Spears, and easily moved around the ring out of his way.

After that incident, Spears lightened up on Don and they became great friends. Any normal person can be pushed into a fight or provoked to anger.

A heavyweight boxer named Bobo and Warren Williams were lifelong friends. They had lived next door to each other as children in Memphis. Bobo was a few years older than Williams and had been his mentor while he was growing up. Bobo was the first to take him to a boxing gym when he was a teenager. Both were professional heavyweight boxers. Williams had been good enough as an amateur to be on the USA Boxing Team and was rated No. 2 in the nation as an amateur. Both boxers were big men: Bobo was a 6-foot-6, 275 pound heavyweight and Williams was 6-foot-1 and 240 pounds.

While sparring with Keith McKnight, Bobo took a clean punch to the eye and suffered a painful injury. Bobo went to the dressing room and placed a feminine hygiene pad (they are used by many boxers to protect their hands in training) above his eye and wrapped the pad with a boxer's red hand wrap. Bobo emerged from the dressing room with the self-designed bandage that looked ridiculous. Williams began to make fun of Bobo, telling him he looked like a sissy. Bobo became very angry which, in turn, angered Williams. Williams started screaming at Bobo and a shoving match ensued. Bobo grabbed a wooden stand that was used to do push-ups on as a weapon and threatened Williams with the deadly club. Immediately, Keith McKnight, Ken Atkin and I tried to separate the two huge men while both traded stinging insults with each other. It became an ugly shoving match. Fortunately, we were able to keep them from hurting each other; however, this incident created hard feelings between the two, and it was many months before they would even speak to one another.

Don't Throw in The Towel!

Vince Lombardi, the late, great Green Bay Packers' National Football coach, once said, "When the going gets tough, the tough get going." That is a great statement, and one that I try to live by. But there are times when trouble comes and then comes again and again.

Life sometimes gets very, very tough. It is so oppressive it beats people down and they are ready to give up and commit suicide.

Maybe you've lost your job, your business is failing, you are facing bankruptcy, you have a child addicted to drugs or in jail, you've been diagnosed with a terrible illness or you've lost a loved one in death. You're on a downhill spiral and have been there for months or maybe even years. Life seems overwhelming and you are beaten, weary and depressed. You can't face your neighbor, let alone your circumstances. There are times in life when you cannot cope. I've been there and have the scars to prove it. Life ain't easy!

When my first wife, Diane, was diagnosed with breast cancer, the news was devastating to me. The weight of this news exerted such pressure on my mind and body that the strain sometimes caused my legs to buckle. I couldn't hold my body erect. I would try to walk, and my legs would not stay under me. This intense force felt like it would at times compress my body flat as a pancake. I was panic-stricken and filled with fear.

I would go into the woods alone, find a secluded spot and get down on my knees. I prayed for her, and I asked the Lord to comfort both of us. This dark, dark cloud had descended upon us and I could feel its ominous presence smothering and choking the life out of us.

In the midst of the storm, I still had to get up every day, go to work, pay bills and face life's challenges. I was my wife's caregiver and, as such, I couldn't devote the time

I needed to my job as a commercial insurance agent. My production fell off; eventually, I was fired. It was almost unbearable for me. I went through this valley of fear and stress for 18 months before the cloud lifted and I felt some relief. At times, I wanted to die in order to be relieved of this stress. But suicide wasn't an option because of my faith in Christ.

After three years, the cancer returned, along with the fear and stress that goes with terminal illnesses. Diane fought a hard fight and lived for four years even though the breast cancer had metastasized before it had been discovered in her body. I felt so helpless because there was nothing I could do to save her. Diane went home to be with the Lord in October 2001.

After she passed away, the days were very dark and dreary for me. I was extremely sad and felt so alone. Several weeks after her death, I drove to Florida to visit my mom and dad.

While in Florida, I couldn't sit still. I needed to be on the move so I drove around the state by myself for a couple of days. I couldn't enjoy the beauty around me because of Diane's passing and the realization that I was truly now alone. My lovely wife was gone.

I sat by a Gulf Coast harbor and noticed a flock of beautiful green parrots playing in front of my feet. As I looked up, I also noticed a swarm of dolphins swimming close by in the bay. It saddened me even more to realize I was witnessing this incredible beauty by myself. There was no one to enjoy it with.

Early the next morning, I went jogging on St. Petersburg beach. I finished my run, and as I walked back to my car a lady of the night pulled into the parking space next to my vehicle. She motioned to me and when I looked her way I noticed her blouse was completely open and she was wearing nothing underneath. She smiled and shook her breasts at me.

Fight The Good Fight

As I looked at her, I instantly remembered the words to a Dwight Yoakum song: "I'm lonely, but I ain't that lonely yet."

I waved her off and got into my car and drove away. I crossed a large bridge that connected the island to the mainland and briefly thought I should stop the car and jump from the bridge to my death. Instantly, I realized my daughter Christy and granddaughter Cambryn still were alive and were precious to me and I needed to be here for them.

The knowledge that I still needed to be here for someone else gave me the strength not to quit. With this knowledge, I was able to move on and not quit. Someone once said, "You may not be somebody in this world. But to somebody you might be the world."

Someone in this world needs you so don't give up and don't quit.

First Steps in a New Direction

Many of us have tried to turn a new leaf in life, or to start with a clean slate, only to fail miserably. It's like a diet or a New Year's resolution that's short term. That happens because we can't change what we are deep down inside.

Only Christ can change the heart. If we are willing to turn away from our sinful nature, Christ can enter our lives and make a new creature out of us. First and foremost there has to be a desire and a willingness inside each of us to want Christ to take control of our lives. If you are willing to give your life completely to Him, then He can change your life.

Addictions are so strong that many Christians are in bondage to them and struggle with them daily. Things like overeating can be just as harmful as alcohol, drug or sexual addictions. However, the perception is that alcohol, drug or sexual addictions are really sinful while overeating is not.

If you have alcohol, drug or sexual addictions that control your life, you've got to get help or these things will destroy you and your family members.

There is absolutely nothing wrong with seeking help if you are in bondage to any addiction.

Recognize you are a sinner. Admit it to God. Say the following: "God I realize I am a sinner; please forgive me of my sin."

Realize that you can't save yourself. "God I realize that Jesus died to save me and that I cannot save myself from sin or even my addictive behavior."

Surrender your life to Christ and allow the Holy Spirit to make a new creature out of you. Say the following: "Lord, I surrender my life totally and completely to Jesus Christ. Jesus I invite you into my life. Come in and make a new creature out of me."

Dealing with Addictions

I once talked to a man about him and his wife devoting their lives to Christ. "Oh, we are good people; we don't need that. Christianity and the church are for people who are bad," he said.

I went to Tennessee Temple University when Paul Wrenn was in seminary there in the 1970s. Paul was one of the world's strongest men. He once held the world record in the squat. At that time, his best lift and record was about 979 pounds. Today's record for the squat is more than 1,000 pounds.

Paul was also an evangelist who traveled all across the country performing feats of strength. One of the feats he performed was to lie on his back and place a concrete block on his stomach. He would then allow someone to take a sledgehammer and smash the block on his stomach. I had the privilege of using the sledgehammer to crush one of those blocks while it rested on his huge stomach in a church service.

Paul and I became friends and he would occasionally come by the Health Club that I owned and perform incredible feats of strength, then tell folks in attendance about the love of Jesus Christ. Paul spent a great deal of time involved in prison ministry. He once said to me he had more converts to Christ in prison than anywhere else. He said. that the reason for this was that people in prison knew that they were sinners and needed help.

Friend, if you feel that nothing is wrong with you and you do not have a problem, then none of this will be of any help to you. The first step in receiving help is in recognizing that you have a problem and that you are out of control.

There is no help for the homosexual who thinks his sin is no more than a loving relationship or that he is just living an alternate lifestyle until he recognizes his or her sin.

Pastor/teacher John MacArthur of Grace Community Church in Sun Valley, California, said, "The worst thing we can do for the homosexual is to call their behavior an alternate lifestyle. If you call it an alternate lifestyle and not a sin, there is no way of salvation."

The same is true for heterosexuals who live together in a loving relationship outside of marriage. There is no difference in God's eyes; they are both fornication. God's word declares that fornicators will not be in heaven.

"Do you not know that the unrighteous will not inherit the kingdom of God? Do not be deceived. Neither fornicators, nor idolaters, nor adulterers, nor homosexuals, nor sodomites, nor thieves, nor covetous, nor drunkards, nor revilers, nor extortioners will inherit the kingdom of God. And such were some of you. But you were washed, but you were sanctified, but you were justified in the name of the Lord Jesus and by the spirit of our God." 1 Corinthians 6: 9-11

There was a time in my life when many of the above terms described me. However, I gave my life to Jesus Christ and He changed me from a vile person into a God-fearing Christian. He washed my sin and me in His blood and made a new creature out of me. He sanctified me or set me apart to glorify Him and He justified me when He saved me. That word justified simply means that when God looks at me he sees me as someone who never sinned. When He looks at a person who has given their life to Jesus Christ, all He sees is the blood shed by Christ to save that individual. He sees a person who has been washed and made clean of their sin by the sacrificial blood of Jesus Christ.

You have to explain away God or throw the Bible out the window to live what the Bible calls an unrighteous lifestyle and believe that you are without sin. The Bible says, *"The wrath of God is revealed from heaven against all ungodliness and unrighteousness of men, who suppress the truth in unrighteousness."* Romans 1:18

According to the Bible, people who live this type of profligate lifestyle know they are doing wrong, but they suppress the truth or explain it away to justify the way they are living. " *Because what may be known of God is manifest in them, for God has shown it to them.*" Romans 1:19

If there is no absolute moral law, then why do we put people in jail in the first place? If it's OK to have a homosexual relationship or an adulterous relationship, then why isn't it OK to kill someone? Why isn't it OK to rob or steal from someone? Where does this sense of morality come from?

The Bible teaches that we all have knowledge of God written inside of us. "*Because although they knew God, they did not glorify him as God.*" Romans 1:21

God has planted a sense of morality into our genetic code. There are those who have become futile in their thoughts and "*their foolish hearts were darkened. Professing themselves to be wise, they became fools.*" Romans 1:21, 22

Those who want to live immoral lifestyles have decided for themselves they will have no God tell them what to do. They reject God and they simply explain away the word of God. These people do one of two things: They deny the very existence of God by declaring there is no God. They will make statements like "You can't tell me what's right or wrong. How dare you to try and place your standard of morality on me or anyone else."

Or, in the second rationalization, folks design their own God. They use man's wisdom to rationalize that "I think that God is a loving God. He loves me so he wouldn't punish me for living the way I do."

God has given us an instruction manual on life called the Bible. This book has stood the test of time. It is a collection of 66 books, written in the course of 1,500 years in Hebrew, Greek and Aramaic. It was written in times of war and in times of peace, and God used about 40 different authors to pen His word. He used kings and shepherds, rich men and poor. It covers many controversial subjects, yet from beginning to end it has one harmonious and continuous theme about God's creation of man: man's ultimate fall and redemption. There are hundreds of prophecies in it that have come true years after the Bible said that they would happen. Men have tried to burn, to outlaw and to kill the very word of God without success. If you want to deny it, reject it, insert your own belief system into it or explain it away, then where will you go for the eternal salvation of your own soul? This is humanity's owner's manual. God declares the only way to receive eternal life in this book. There is no help and no hope for you if you reject the Bible and ultimately Jesus Christ. *"Jesus said to him, I am the way, the truth, and the life. No one comes to the Father except through me."* John 14:6

When a person gives their life to Christ, they let go of things that ruled their life before they became a Christian. I've seen people accept Christ and instantly give up immoral lifestyles, smoking, drinking and drugs without any problem. For others, those addictive lifestyles aren't that easy to quit. Rev. Al Henson, my dear friend and former pastor, said, "Becoming a Christian and giving up addictive habits is similar to being on a boat that lands at shore. The closer you are to the boat, the easier it is to get back in and go for a ride. The longer you are away from the boat and the more distant you are from it the easier it is to stay away from it." It takes time to change.

Murdered at the Krooked Knite Tavern

Michael Jackson was a very gifted athlete, standing 6-foot-7 and weighing 235 pounds. He was a basketball star and the leading scorer at Bradford High School, where he scored 371 points in his senior year. He was a black belt in karate and also owned a karate studio in Kenosha. We went to the same high school, grew up together and were casual friends. Whenever we would bump into each other in one of the local bars, he would throw playful punches at me (although he was a foot taller) and ask, "How's the boxing going?"

I would tell him what was going on with me and ask him about his martial arts. He was always very gracious, friendly and polite.

On a cold New Year's Eve, Michael was celebrating at a tavern in Kenosha. The clock rolled past midnight and into the New Year. Around 2:30 a.m., two women in the bar got into a fight. According to police reports, Michael had broken up the fight.

Michael and a couple of guys named Anthony and James got into an argument. A confrontation ensued, and James was told to leave the tavern; he and his friend Anthony left. A few minutes later, Michael also walked outside and began arguing with James, who walked away, but then Anthony started to argue with Michael.

Witnesses told police the two exchanged heated words and shots were fired. Michael was first hit in the side and a couple of other times in the chest as he chased his assailant. Only 26, he died on that cold, dark, frozen street in front of the Krooked Knite Tavern.

Witnesses at the tavern identified the suspects to police, who obtained a search warrant. Just before 5 a.m., they knocked on the door of the house where Anthony and James resided. James answered the knock and opened the side door to the house. The police went upstairs and found the killer, Anthony, sound asleep in his bed. A pistol with three spent cartridges also was found in the house.

I was devastated to hear about the violent death of such a promising and gifted man, whom I considered a friend. I was amazed and shocked that the killer had so little remorse that he was able to sleep without any concern for the one whose life he had just taken. Some people are so wicked that their conscience is totally seared and they feel no emotion. Their conscience has been burned beyond feeling just as if they had been branded with a red-hot branding iron.

Wildcat Whiskey

Woodrow Pharr, my cousin, lived in Alabama, my birthplace. Woodrow was a bootlegger and had an illegal moonshine still on Jack Davis' property. As a trade-off to using his land for the still, Woodrow supplied Davis with whiskey.

This local homebrew is almost pure alcohol, and is so strong that it is called "Wildcat" in this rural part of the state. Jack had been in an alcohol rehabilitation program and Woodrow had driven him home several days earlier. He was craving alcohol. He had asked Woodrow to bring him some whiskey when he came to his house that day. Woodrow and a couple of his friends arrived to work on the still.

Jack opened his front screen door, stuck his head out and asked Woodrow, "Did you bring that stuff I asked you to bring?" Woodrow answered, "No!"

A couple of minutes later, Jack hollered and asked Woodrow to come into the house.

When Woodrow walked in the front door of the house, Jack was waiting on the other side of the room with a deer rifle in his hands. He shot Woodrow in the stomach three times, killing him almost instantly. Woodrow had raised his hand to helplessly try to shield his body; one of the bullets severed one of his fingers.

This cold-blooded murder was so sad and tragic: Sad because Woodrow was only 33 years of age and had a wife and three young children waiting for him at home and tragic because his mother and grandmother were devout Christian women and he had been raised in church. He had heard the story many times of how God had sent his son Jesus to die for our sin. Yet, when it came time for him to depart this life, my own first cousin had very little time to prepare for eternity.

We all have an appointment with death and judgment. *"It is appointed for men to die once, but after this the judgment."*

Fight The Good Fight

(Hebrews 9:27). Nothing will keep us from this appointment with death when our time comes to go.

There's a story of a minister who waited in line to have his car filled with gas just before a long holiday weekend. The attendant worked quickly, but there were many cars ahead of him in front of the service station. Finally the attendant motioned him toward a vacant pump. "I'm sorry, reverend, about the delay but it's as if everyone waits until the last minute to get ready for a long trip."

The minister chuckled, I know what you mean. It's the same in my business."

We all have this idea that we will live a long life and still have enough time to make peace with our Maker while we are lying on our deathbed. There is something inside each of us that's makes us believe that we've got plenty of time to worry about spiritual things later. Yet, death overtakes many of us suddenly and quickly without notice or warning. Some folks die instantly and don't have even one minute in which they can pray.

Therefore the most important thing in life should be to prepare for death ahead of time. Zig Ziglar, the renowned motivational speaker and born-again Christian, has said, "We are going to be dead a lot longer than we're alive."

There is life after death that lasts for eternity. There is a heaven and a hell. Heaven is a place of perfect peace and complete joy. Hell is a place of everlasting punishment reserved for Satan and his followers. Doesn't it make sense to prepare for eternity? Don't put off till tomorrow what you know you should do today. Consider the following Bible verse:

Hebrews 2:3: *"How shall we escape if we neglect so great a salvation?"*

Chapter 6: Advice for the New Christian

A King's Instruction for Facing Life's Battles

It's not easy to face a legendary boxing champion. Most people do not have that type of courage. Few people would accept such a challenge if it was offered to them, but Ken "The Bull" Atkin was an exception. He chose to fight the great champion Thomas "Hit Man" Hearns. Sometime in life, almost everyone is presented with a giant battle that they would not have chosen for themselves. Unfortunately, we end up right in the middle of life-threatening circumstances, whether we're ready for them or not.

When trials and tribulations arrive on our doorstep, we may not have the strength or courage to deal with them. It's easy for those on the outside looking in to tell us what to do or how to be courageous in our battles, just as it was easy for me to sit in the safety of our corner outside of the boxing ring to tell Atkin how to fight the dangerous champion. But he was the one who had to have the strength and courage to fight the battle.

We don't understand how or why we are faced with these battles, but life is full of them. King Solomon, the wisest man who ever lived, gave some great advice on dealing with adversity. In Proverbs 3:5-6, he said, *"Trust in the Lord with all your heart and lean not on your own understanding. In all your ways acknowledge him, and he shall direct your paths."*

In our lifetimes, most of us will face a battle that we can't handle on our own. It might be too overwhelming for you to face by yourself. . You may not understand why it's happening to you and it might be the most painful experience you'll ever face.

When trials and tribulations come your way, put your faith and trust in the Lord. Don't rely on reason or only earthly understanding. You might get battered and bruised along the way, but acknowledge the Lord and he will guide you through the storm and bring you through the fire.

How Can I Keep From Losing Heart?

The Apostle Paul encouraged the Christians at Corinth not to lose courage. He told them:

"Since we have this ministry, as we have received mercy, we do not lose heart." (2 Corinthians 4:1)

I've heard boxers say many times that to win a boxing match you have to take your opponent's heart away. The way to beat and destroy someone is to make them lose heart or to make them quit. The meaning of the Greek term "lose heart" in the Bible refers to abandoning oneself to cowardly surrender. The Apostle Paul is telling us that, as Christians, we have received mercy, we have been forgiven of our sins, and we have this ministry, so we must not lose heart.

"Go into all the world and preach the Gospel to every creature," Christ commanded us in Mark 16:15. Every Christian's ministry is to proclaim the gospel of Jesus Christ as we go about our daily lives. Similarly, 2 Corinthians 4: 7 tells us, *"We have this treasure in earthen vessels, that the excellence of the power may be of God and not of us."*

We are earthen vessels created out of clay, like pottery. The Holy Spirit is the treasure that dwells inside of those vessels that have received Christ as savior. The treasure isn't the vessel, but rather it is God's Spirit, which dwells inside of the vessel. The power to not lose heart comes from the Spirit dwelling inside of the vessel.

With God and his grace, there is a very real power in us, the vessels. Satan and his demons are very real and dangerous spiritual opponents. These evil forces constantly look for ways to break us down emotionally, spiritually and physically. We have to call on God for his strength and power to defeat these forces that seek to destroy us. The power is in God's Holy Spirit, which dwells inside us.

Twice in 2 Corinthians 4 the Apostle Paul tells us not to lose heart. First, he says in 2 Corinthians 4:1, *"As we have received mercy, we do not lose heart."*

Then he explains that life is sometimes unbearably tough. Humanly, we don't have the strength to go on:

"We are hard-pressed on every side, yet not crushed; we are perplexed, but not in despair; persecuted, but not forsaken; struck down, but not destroyed - always carrying about in the body the dying of the Lord Jesus, that the life of Jesus also may be manifested in our body." (2 Corinthians 4:8-10).

Here's the bottom line: Life is tough. Sometimes it's excruciatingly tough. But Paul assures us that our trouble in this life is momentary and light in comparison to the glory we will receive as servants of Jesus Christ for eternity in Heaven.

"Endurance is based on one's ability to look beyond the physical to the spiritual; beyond the present to the future, and beyond the visible to the invisible," said Dr. John MacArthur, Author and Editor of the MacArthur study Bible and one of the great bible teachers of our day.

"We do not look at the things which are seen, but at the things which are not seen. For the things which are seen are temporary, but the things which are not seen are eternal." (2 Corinthians 4:18).

The physical life is only temporary. It is not eternal. The spiritual things that we do not see are real, but invisible to us. The spiritual things are eternal.

The gospel in a nutshell is that Christ died for our sins, was buried and rose again. This is a historical fact, and it is what separates Christianity apart from all religions: We have a living savior. He's alive. He's alive because God the father raised him from the dead. The Bible declares,

"He who raised up the Lord Jesus will also raise us with Jesus." (2 Corinthians 4:14)

If God has the power to raise Him up, He certainly has the power to do what He said He would do and raise us up, also. The Bible also gives us another beautiful picture of what transpires at death. A seed planted in the grown must die to produce life in the form of a beautiful new plant.

"Therefore we do not lose heart, Even though our outward man is perishing, yet the inward man is being renewed day by day." (2 Corinthians 4:16)

I'm sure that facing death is not an easy thing to do. I'm conscious of the fact that I'm not getting any younger. Life is a fleeting thing; it comes and goes very quickly. I'm not certain that I will have the strength or courage to face it when my time comes. What I am certain of is that God's grace will see me through. I believe and hold to these precious promises given to us in God's Holy Bible. Do not lose heart.

How Can We Prepare For Eternal Life?

Jesus said to Nicodemus, a ruler of the Jews, *"Most assuredly I say to you, unless one is born again he cannot see the kingdom of God."* (John 3:3)

This confused Nicodemus and he questioned Jesus about it. Jesus replied, *"You must be born again"*. (John 3:7b)

Jesus went on to explain to Nicodemus that God sent his only son into the world that the world through Him (Jesus) might be saved. (John 3:16-17).

Simply said, God sent his only son Jesus to earth to die a sacrificial death for mankind. Those who believe in Him and receive his gift of salvation will be rewarded with eternal life in a place God calls Heaven. The Bible describes Heaven as a place of untold happiness, peace and joy.

Death for the believer in Christ offers tremendous hope for eternity. There still is fear in the process of dying for a Christian, but there is a knowledge that you are going to a better place and a better life.

In January 2004, I visited my good friend Benny Benson, a believer in Christ, who was in his 70s and had terminal cancer. Benny was originally from Oklahoma and I sat with him and we watched the Oklahoma football team play for the national championship that night. "Benny," I asked. "How are you doing emotionally with the news the Doctors have given you? "Well, I know where I am going," he replied.

He had a complete and total confidence that when he died he was going to go to heaven. This faith that his eternity was secure allowed him to function and live confidently those last few weeks of his life. He was even able to sit and enjoy watching his team play football. A short time later Benny died and based on the word of God, he went immediately into the presence of the Lord.

Receiving Christ today is as simple as praying the following prayer:

Fight The Good Fight

Father, I come to you today and ask you to forgive me of my sin, Thank you for sending your son Jesus to die for me, Lord Jesus I accept your sacrificial gift and ask you to come into my life and be my Lord and Savior, in Jesus name I pray. Amen.

If you sincerely prayed that simple prayer, the Bible declares that you are now saved and are a child of God. "If you confess with your mouth the Lord Jesus and believe in your heart that God has raised him from the dead, you will be saved. (Romans 10:9).

I encourage you to find a Bible-based church and start attending services. Start reading the Bible. A good place to begin is in the book of John. Read that book over and over again until you have a good understanding of what's happened in your life now that you have invited the Savior to take control over your life. Tell others that you have given your life to Christ and trust that you are eternally secure in the master's hand. May the Lord richly bless your new life in Him.

Sorrow Not, Have Hope

There was a man who was member of our church that lost his wife to cancer. This man was in his 40s and went through a tremendous amount of grief. He would come to church and begin crying at every service. His wife was a Christian and so was he, but he could not find comfort to ease her loss. This went on for a couple of years, which seemed to be an inordinate amount of time. His public display of grief went on for so long that others would roll their eyes and make negative comments about him whenever he would start to cry.

The Apostle Paul wrote to the early church believers in Thessalonica that also were grieving because of the death of their saved loved ones. Paul encouraged them not to sorrow as others who have no hope.

My wife Lanita lost her first husband Steve, two of her children and her father in death. I lost Diane, my first wife of 32 years, to breast cancer and recently my father. Obviously, we grieved after losing our loved ones and we dearly miss them now.

My dear friends Ben and Ermeda Chapman, the founders of Lighthouse Christian Camp in Smithville, Tennessee, lost their son Justin to a reoccurrence of cancer when he was in his early 20s. The disease first occurred when Justin was an adolescent, but he survived and lived long enough to grow into manhood. It hurt Ben and Ermeda deeply, but it almost consumed and destroyed Ben. It was several years before Ben was able to overcome this oppressive grief. Justin was a dynamic Christian. He and my daughter Christy were dear friends growing up.

Justin's death hurt everyone who knew him and the family. After his death, everyone was concerned about Ben because the loss of his son was overwhelming. Although he still misses Justin immensely, Ben is busy working at the camp today helping underprivileged children come to know the Lord. There is no way of knowing how many thousands of young children Ben and Ermeda have ministered to or that have been saved as a result of their camp ministry. They lost their oldest son temporarily, but God has given them thousands of children in the Lord that they will spend eternity with in Heaven's glory. This is a great ministry worthy of support. If you want to give to a great work of God here is their address: Lighthouse Christian Camp, 205 Serenity Place, Smithville, TN 37166. This year (2007) will mark the 25th year of ministry to disadvantaged children.

A pastor asked the following question in one of his messages. "Why do we grieve?" He then said, "Grieving is the price you pay for loving someone. The more you love them the more you grieve when you lose them."

Losing a child has to be the hardest thing to experience in life. The grief you experience must feel like it will devour you. But with God's help, you can heal from the wounds of losing a dear loved one.

Paul explained to the church in Thessalonica that they didn't need to continually be in sorrow because their saved loved ones were with the Lord. *"But I do not want you to be ignorant, brethren, concerning those who have fallen asleep, lest you sorrow as others who have no hope."* (1Thessalonians 4:13)

Notice that sorrow is only for those who have no hope. Sorrow is for those who don't believe that Jesus died and rose again. Paul refers to believers who have died as having fallen asleep, for those who know the Lord as their Savior death is similar to sleep. The physical body is dead, but not the soul. The soul and spirit are alive and conscious.

Biblical scholar Dr. John MacArthur said, "But there is no reason for Christians to sorrow when a brother dies as if some great loss to that person has come."

They have completed their life on earth but are alive for evermore in heaven. Life follows death. That's why Jesus referred to death as sleep because it is not the end it is only a change. The Bible tells us *"to be absent from the body is to be present with the Lord."* (2 Corinthians 5:8)

The Apostle Paul said that *"For to me, to live is Christ, and to die is gain.* (Philippians 1:21)

Paul's purpose for living was to serve Christ. He understood that death would relieve him of earthly trials and tribulations. He knew that when he died he would be with Christ. He understood that he would have intimate, conscious fellowship with Christ and other believers.

Paul said that his desire was to leave this earthly life to be with Christ. He knew that dying and going to Heaven would be far better than living this life of pain, sorrow and death.

My pastor, Dr. Jack Graham, said, "There is a hunger in the heart for Heaven. Heaven is a real place, more real than where we are today." In his book titled Heaven, Randy Alcorn said. "Heaven is home. People say that when a Christian dies they are leaving home. They're not leaving home. They're going home."

In his lifetime, Paul had been stoned and left for death. He talks about knowing a man who had been caught up into the third heaven, the abode of God. He explained that this person saw unspeakable things while there. Many Biblical scholars believe that it was Paul himself who had caught a glimpse of Heaven while he was still alive.

Could it be that the Apostle Paul saw heaven's glory and that is why he had absolutely no fear of death? He actually wanted to die so he could be in heaven instead of on earth. He said that the only reason for him to stay on earth was for the benefit of his fellow Christians. God used him to preach the Gospel all over the Roman Empire. The Apostle Paul founded most of the early churches. Paul had work that needed to be completed before his departure. When he completed what God had for him to do, God called him home to heaven.

Fight The Good Fight

In his book *Confessions of A Happy Christian*, Zig Ziglar tells the story of his friend Les Mills, who was pronounced clinically dead by a doctor. Twenty minutes after the doctor had pronounced him dead, a nurse walked into his room and detected signs of life.

Later that evening, Les Mills sat on the side of his bed talking to his wife, friends and pastor He told them about the wonderful life he had experienced in the brief 15 months he had been a Christian. He said to his wife, "I don't want you crying for me. I know I'm going to be with the Lord and as you can see, heaven is a beautiful place."

He then went on to describe things he had seen in heaven and was quite puzzled why his wife Evelyn didn't remember seeing them, because she was with him, he said. His wife, his pastor and his friend Zig Ziglar believe that he had seen heaven in those 20 minutes after the doctor had pronounced him dead.

Ziglar said that the next morning, he breathed his last breath and went home to be with the Lord.

I heard a pastor recently tell a story of a 92-year-old Christian woman who had lost all of her friends. She said, "I hope I die soon, because all of my friends have died and are in heaven and they will think I didn't make it."

King David experienced the death of one of his children when the child was only seven days old. David fasted and prayed for the child for the seven days of his life. After the child passed away, David stopped praying and asked his servants to prepare food for him to eat. His servants asked him why he ate nothing for those seven days but wanted to eat after the child died. King David explained that he couldn't bring the child back again.

He said, *"I shall go to him, but he shall not return to me."* (2 Samuel 12:22).

David recognized that he would be reunited with his son in heaven after his own death. Be comforted and know that

Fight The Good Fight

there will be a reuniting with Christian family members that have gone on before us.

David understood that a saint or an innocent child who died "was gathered to his people." This was said of Abraham, Isaac, Aaron and Moses. The Old Testament declares that their souls and spirits were reunited in a place called Abraham's bosom, or paradise.

There is no need for a Christian who has lost a believing loved one to be without hope. Ziglar tells of losing his daughter Susan to cancer when she was in her 30s. After her death, he went home and tried to sleep that night but wasn't able to. So he arose from bed in the middle of the night and began to pray. He put a Bill Gaither gospel video in the VCR and watched Vestal Goodman sing. During his time of prayer, the Lord assured him that Susan was home with him in heaven and that she was OK. This assurance gave Zig the peace and strength to go on. He returned to bed and slept peacefully the rest of the night. In his hour of need, God provided comfort.

Our saved loved ones are with the Lord. There is no safer place in all of creation than to be with the Creator himself. Some people have an extremely hard time of letting go of their grief. They feel they have lost their loved one forever. But as Christians, we will see our saved loved ones again. We will spend eternity with them in a place where there is no sickness, disease, crime, pain, suffering or death. I know I'll see my loved ones again. If God were to grant me an extra long life, I'll still see my loved ones who have gone on before me in the next 20 or 30 years. That length of time is just a blink of an eye in comparison to eternity

Those who are alive when Christ returns for his church will be reunited with their loved ones in the air. *"For if we believe that Jesus died and rose again, even so God will bring with him those who sleep in Jesus."* (1 Thessalonians 4:14)

Those who sleep in Jesus are those Christians who have passed away previously. *"For this we say to you by the word of the Lord, that we who are alive and remain until the coming of the Lord will by no means precede those who are asleep. "For the Lord himself will descend from heaven with a shout, with the voice of an archangel, and with the trumpet of God. And the dead in Christ will rise first. Then we who are alive and remain shall be caught up together with them in the clouds to meet the Lord in the air. And thus we shall always be with the Lord. Therefore comfort one another with these words."* (1 Thessalonians 4:15-18)

Notice that Paul said that this is the word of the Lord and that those who are asleep in Jesus will have their bodies resurrected. Then we will be caught up together with them and meet them in the air. He further explains that from that moment on we will forever be with the Lord and our loved ones. Paul encourages us to comfort one another with these words. This is something to shout about! This is referred to in the Bible as the Blessed Hope of the believer.

If you have lost a saved loved one and can't get over it, be comforted in knowing you will see them again if you know Christ as your savior.

I recently noticed a church billboard sign as I drove by that said, "Sunset in one place is sunrise in another place." I believe this is a Biblically correct assessment of a Christian's time on earth. When the sun sets on our life and we depart this earth, we instantly are ushered into the light of a heavenly sunrise where there will be no more sunsets and no more night. We will forever be with Jesus, the light of the world.

Finding Relief from Grief

Recognize that grief is normal and the time needed for healing is different for each person.

Ask God to consume you with His love and to comfort you in your time of need.

Ask Christian friends to pray for you in your lost. Join a grief support group. People with similar needs will bond with you instantly and will pray for you fervently.

Remember These Things

Our saved loved one's who have died, are with the Lord in a perfectly peaceful place where they are enjoying life fully. They are alive for evermore. As believers in Christ, we will be reunited with them.

As Christians, regardless of our circumstances here on earth, we have a blessed hope. We are going to leave this life of pain, suffering and sorrow some day and spend eternity in heaven with our wonderful Lord and Savior and millions of Christian brothers and sisters in the Lord.

Whatever pain we have experienced here on earth will be completely gone and forgotten in heaven. Earth has no sorrow that God in heaven will not heal.

Sorrow is for those who have NO HOPE! Christians are people of hope. Our home for eternity is heaven and we will know our loved ones who are there and they will recognize and know us as well. When Jesus was on the mount of Transfiguration with Moses and Elijah both had been dead for centuries. Yet, the apostles recognized them. They knew who they were. They were still Moses and Elijah.

Cheer up! We're going home to be with Jesus some sweet day.

Dealing with Anger

There's an old saying in boxing: "Lose your temper, lose the fight." Boxing is a sport in which the great boxers are extremely relaxed and show no emotion. Their movement is very fluid and smooth. These fighters are like great poker players who you can't read. They have a poker face. The great boxer shows no emotion in his face. You can't tell what he's thinking or which punch he is about to throw at you. Boxers who are angry become very tight and flinch before they throw a punch. The angry boxer will telegraph every move he makes and a relaxed boxer will elude everything an angry opponent tries to do and will pick them apart.

The Bible says that we are not to sin when we get angry. *"Be angry, and do not sin: do not let the sun go down on your wrath."* (Ephesians 4:26)

I've sure blown that one many times in my life. Uncontrolled anger creates problems it doesn't settle them. We have a God-given right to defend ourselves. If someone is trying to physically harm you or your family, you have every right to defend yourself. But getting angry with someone about some minor incident doesn't help. You can't be angry and be reasonable at the same time. When a person is angry, they are totally out of control. They can't think rationally or reasonably because of the emotional anger.

"Scrap Iron" Johnson cracked his own skull while he was angry and tried to hurt his opponent. A young boxer almost got seriously hurt because I was frustrated and angry with him when he wouldn't do what I asked him to do. The bullying parent angered the boxer who retaliated and almost set off World War III in our gym. Lifelong friends Warren and Bobo were about to seriously hurt each other because a minor incident got out of hand.

Anger is a normal feeling we experience when someone has wronged us. Unresolved anger can turn into bitterness, which can lead to hatred of those who have wronged us. This in turn leads to unforgiveness. The Bible teaches that if we want God to forgive our sins, we have to be willing to forgive others when they have wronged us. (Matthew 6:14)

The real problem with anger is that it causes harm to the person who is angry. Some people have been hurt so deeply that it is hard for them to forgive and to forget. Anger and bitterness cause emotional problems for those who harbor these feeling of resentment or hate. The real issue is healing. If you are an angry person who wants emotional or physical healing, you must let go of that anger and forgive those who have wronged you so God can forgive you of your sin and provide emotional or physical healing for you.

A daughter sits in a jail cell today because of unresolved anger and trauma in her life. I met her when she was 21. She's now 25, but it all began when she was just 4 and her father was killed in an accident. As a child, she was angry about the loss of her father and probably angry with God for allowing it to happen. As an adolescent, she began to show behavioral problems. She started to get into trouble in school. She started smoking and doing drugs at 13 and began to hang around a very rough crowd.

She also began getting into trouble with the law and was totally out of control and even stole a car. Another time she stole a car that belonged to her older siblings and had a wreck and totaled the vehicle. Her mother didn't know what to do with her, so when she was 14 years old she sent her to a home for wayward girls hoping that this would help her. Instead, it angered her even more. After getting out of the girls' home a year later, her behavioral problems worsened.

In her late teens, she began to get arrested for drug possession, and was in and out of jail on a regular basis. She dated a young man, became pregnant and they got married. A precious daughter was born. Because of her unresolved problems and her out-of-control behavior, the marriage ended a couple of years later. She had a job, so she and the daughter moved into an apartment, but she sank deeper and deeper into an alcohol- and drug-addicted lifestyle.

She was living very destructively and would stay high or drunk for days at a time. She wasn't able to care for the child, so the husband went to court and gained custody of the little girl. This caused tremendous anger and resentment from the mother. She became very bitter about losing her child and soon she lost her job and all she had. She went deeply into debt and had no job or income. Whenever she would get a job, she would lose it in three days because she would show up at work drunk or not show up at all.

She began sleeping wherever she could. Sometimes she would stay with drunk or drug- addicted men who abused her even more. Other times she lived on the streets. She got arrested again, and her mother spent several thousand dollars on lawyers to keep her from going to prison. She was released from jail and immediately returned to her decadent lifestyle.

Soon she was arrested again, and spent several months in jail then in an alcohol and drug rehab facility. After leaving there, she was back on the streets living the same way as before. Later, she was sent to a state hospital for several months. Upon release, she returned to alcohol and drugs and the streets again.

She was arrested again and then released. She finally was caught with a felony possession of drugs and was sentenced to two years in prison. The judge released her on parole and she went to another rehab center for a few months, but left it to return to the drugs and alcohol. She was found by construction workers wandering the streets of New Orleans several months after Hurricane Katrina had hit that city. They helped return her to the authorities to get her off of the street. She had violated her probation and is now in jail awaiting a hearing before a judge to determine her plight.

Yes, she has alcohol- and drug-addictive problems, but she is still angry about losing her dad 20 years ago. She's angry about the abuses she suffered as a child. She's angry about being sent to a home as a teenager, she's angry about losing custody of her daughter, she's angry that another young woman is living with her former husband and raising her daughter, she's angry because she's locked up and has nothing. She's angry because she is an outcast and her family won't have anything to do with her. She craves a normal life. She wants to have a home, a family and to be accepted. She's angry at the world, but punishes herself and the ones who love her because she can't control her life.

Steve Troglio, pastor of Eagle Rock Church in Orland Park, Illinois, tells how as an angry young man he almost beat another person to death. He furiously beat a neighbor boy unconscious by smashing his head against a concrete sidewalk. Police pulled him off of the young man and paramedics took the neighbor boy to the hospital. Steve waited several days to see if the hospitalized young man would wake up. Fortunately for Steve, he did wake up without any brain damage.

"I hadn't always been so angry and violet." Steve said.

When Steve was 7, his father's business went under and his dad left home. Several months later, the sheriff evicted his mother, sister and him from their home. His mother then moved them to a city 14 hours away and into a two-bedroom basement apartment in a drug-infested slum. In his new neighborhood, five kids broke his nose and cracked his ribs.

His mother soon turned to drinking. When she got drunk she became violent and would spit on Steve, hit him or throw beer bottles at him. She would also throw him out of the house for days at a time. When that happened, Steve had to stay in abandoned buildings and dig in the trash for something to eat.

"I became incredibly angry, I was like a cocked pistol, ready to fire at the slightest provocation, I guess that's why I responded so violently when that bully started picking on my little sister," Steve said.

As a teenager, Steve dated a girl who told him that God loved him and that he needed to give his life to Christ. He also talked with her parents about Jesus and what it meant to be a Christian. He could see there was something different about them.

"Something so comforting, so inviting," said Steve.

Finally Steve knelt and gave his life to Jesus Christ.

"In the following weeks, God continued to change me. He pointed out lots of things in my life that I needed to give him control of. He also showed me that I needed to forgive my mom."

Steve went to his mother and told her that if he had ever done anything to hurt her he was sorry. "I also want you to know I forgive you," Steve told his mom.

You see, Steve was full of anger, but gave his life to Christ. The Lord showed him that he needed to forgive others who had hurt him. When he was willing to do that, God provided healing for his own tormented mind. Steve was healed emotionally. He overcame this anger in his life and in adulthood became a church pastor. God can change you just like he did Steve Troglio.

There were a couple of boxers I had worked with who I felt had done me wrong. I had trained them as youngsters and had managed their careers when they became professional boxers, and they both went elsewhere shortly after my wife passed away.

I had devoted more than 10 years of my life to each of them. I had traveled all across the country with them. I had spent thousands of dollars on both of them to further their careers. I didn't remember doing anything to them that would have caused such treatment. One morning while I was praying, I felt that God was impressing upon my heart to ask them to forgive me. In my prayer, I rejected the Holy Spirit's prompting.

"No God! I haven't done anything wrong. Why should I ask for forgiveness."

The impression became even stronger. So that very morning, I reluctantly and painfully sat down and wrote the individuals each a letter, asking them to forgive me of any wrong that I had done to them. I'm sure there was something in their minds that I did to them that they perceived was wrong. But because of my pride and presumed innocence it hurt me to write those letters and it hurt me even more to mail them.

I've never heard back from either of them regarding the request for forgiveness. However, those letters freed me from the anger and bitterness that I was harboring against them. I received emotional healing because I was obedient to the Holy Spirit of God telling me to ask for forgiveness, and subsequently I've been able to forgive them even though they have never said they were sorry or asked me to forgive them.

The scripture says, *"Bearing with one another, and forgiving one another, if anyone has a complaint against another; even as Christ forgave you, so you also must do.* (Colossians 3:13)

If Christ forgave you of your sin my dear brother or sister, you also must forgive those who have wronged you. When you forgive someone else you receive healing for yourself.

Maybe you have screwed up your life just as I did mine. Maybe you have been a murderer, an adulterer, a fornicator, a child molester or a homosexual. God bids you to come as you are and give your life to Him. I couldn't change what I was until I was willing to give Christ control of my life. When I gave my life to Him, the Holy Spirit of God moved into my life and began to change me.

After giving my life to Christ something happened to me. The rage inside of me died. The anger I'd experienced most of my life was no longer there. The selfish person who used to get violently angry now loved and cared for others. The self-image problems disappeared. The angry, bitter, brawling young man was now a peacemaker whenever possible. For the next 20 years as a boxing coach, it seemed like I was always soothing ruffled feathers. I was the guy in the middle who was trying to calm down angry men.

I'm so ashamed of the sinful things I did in my early life. For the first 20 or 25 years of my life, I was not a person of honor. I'm so ashamed of that today. I failed in almost everything I did.

Today, I don't even recognize that person. That old person died with Christ on the cross of Calvary.

"Therefore, if anyone is in Christ he is a new creation, old things have passed away; behold all things have become new." (2 Corinthians 5:17)

When I gave my life to Christ, God changed me completely.

I'm not the man I should be. But because of God's grace, I'm certainly not the person I used to be. Today my heart's desire is to be a man of Godly conviction, a man of honor. I want to honor my Lord and Savior Jesus Christ for the rest of my life. I want to love and not hate. I want to give and not take. I want to forgive those who have wronged me and to be forgiven by those I have wronged. I want to lead others to Christ. When I stand before God, I want to hear him say, *"Well done, thy good and faithful servant."*

I thank you Father for your mercy and grace, and for your eternal salvation that you have bestowed upon me.

There are a number of people I hurt in those years while I was living for Satan. I've confessed my sin and have asked God to forgive me, and I've also asked some of those I've offended to forgive me as well. I've lost contact with so many people. If you by some miracle are reading this and I've wronged you and haven't asked for your forgiveness, then I truly am sorry for the wrong I did to you and I ask you to please forgive me. I'm sincerely sorry. I want to have a clear conscience before God and my fellow man. It is sort of like the hit television series *My Name is Earl*. Earl Hickey, the show's protagonist, seeks the many people in his life he did wrong in his earlier days of crime and mischief. After I turned my life to God, I wanted to undo all the wrongs that I had committed. While we may not be able to unring the bell, we can repent and turn to the Lord.

God truly worked a miracle in my life. He can do the same for you. Go to the Lord in prayer and tell him that you've made a mess of your life and that you've sinned against him. Ask him to forgive you and ask him to take control of your life. That's called being born again. Just ask Christ's forgiveness for your sin and then release control of you life to him. You had a physical birth when your mother birthed you. Giving your life to Christ is a new birth. It is a spiritual birth.

Chapter 7: Heavyweight Champions and Would-Be Contenders

Visiting Ali

Having grown up 50 miles north of Chicago I spent much time there. I occasionally trained at the old CYO gym just west of downtown. Larry Freeman and I drove from Wisconsin to watch the incomparable Muhammad Ali train at the old Mayor Daley's Navy Pier gym one beautiful spring day in 1971. The gym was located at the end of the pier, which is approximately 280-foot wide and extends more than one-half mile into Lake Michigan

The self-proclaimed "Greatest of all time" was forced out of boxing by the federal government for refusing to be inducted into the United States Army during the Vietnam War. As he put it, "I ain't got no quarrel with them Vietcong."

Because of legal troubles, the undefeated champion was stripped of his heavyweight championship and wasn't allowed to fight from March 22, 1967, until October 26, 1970.

After his return to boxing, he fought perennial contender Jerry Quarry. In any other era other than the 1970s that included Ali, George Foreman and Joe Frazier, Irish Jerry Quarry, probably would have become a world champion. He was a small heavyweight at 6-foot-1, 195 pounds, but he was a very crafty boxer who could punch with either hand.

Early in the bout, the great Ali, who was too big, fast and skillful, hit Quarry above his left eye, causing a severe cut. In the third round, the referee stopped the bout and Ali was credited with a third-round technical knockout win. In Ali's next bout, he had a rough time with Oscar Bonavena, the durable contender from Argentina, until catching him clean and knocking him out in the 15th round on December 7, 1970. Then, in the "battle of the century," Ali suffered the first loss of his career via a 15-round unanimous decision against the undefeated Smokin' Joe Frazier. Ali was attempting to win back the heavyweight championship that had been taken from him when he refused induction into the United States Army. That fight on March 8, 1971, was voted the *Ring Magazine* Fight of the Year and went down in history as one of the greatest boxing matches ever as both warriors beat each other so fiercely that both of them went to the hospital after the bout. Frazier legitimately whipped Ali and solidified his victory with a sensational knockdown of Ali in the 15th and final round of their first bout. However, Ali also earned a measure of respect for rising from the canvas after tasting the devastating power of Frazier's brutal left hook.

Ali later would redeem himself against Frazier by beating him in 1974 and again in '75 in the classic "Thrilla in Manila." Ali was quoted as saying the fights against Frazier were like a near-death experience. All three fights were voted Fight of the Year by *Ring Magazine*.

After the first Frazier fight in 1971, Ali returned to the gym in the spring to prepare for a summer match against Jimmy Ellis, his boyhood friend, former champion and former sparring partner. Ellis actually had beaten him as an amateur when they were teenagers, but hardly anybody believed he could beat Ali then. He was training in Chicago for his bout at Mayor Richard Daley's foundation gym at Navy Pier on the shore of Lake Michigan.

Jimmy Ellis, left, and Kerry Pharr visit before the Ali-Spinks bout Sept. 15, 1978, in New Orleans.

He was born Cassius Clay and had captured an Olympic Gold medal as a light heavyweight in 1960 in Rome under that name. After winning his first championship by defeating the formidable Sonny Liston in 1964, Clay joined the Nation of Islam and changed his name to Muhammad Ali. He was handsome, flashy, cocky and an incredibly gifted athlete. I wasn't really a fan then; I thought he was a racist because of the way he acted and talked. I believed that he hated white people and that he was no different than a Klansman. I believed then and still do now that Islam is an ungodly religion. But I was fascinated by Ali's skill and boxing ability. In those early days, his speed and mobility were untouchable. He was so fast he could dismantle huge, powerful, skillful heavyweights literally in the blink of an eye. "Float like a butterfly, sting like a bee," – a phrase coined by Drew

Fight The Good Fight

"Bundini" Brown, one of Ali's handlers – described Ali's unbelievable ability.

My friend Larry had won the local Golden Gloves championship for three consecutive years and was called by our local newspaper the "Dean of Boxing."

Larry really had a good eye for boxing talent. He was always betting on fights, and he had an uncanny ability to pick the winner of almost every bout. Larry knew Ali was something special. When the then-Cassius Clay turned professional, Larry made a decision to bet on him on every fight throughout his entire career.

Before Ali's arrival on the fistic scene, fighters were quiet, very polite and civil to each other. Then, Cassius Clay roared onto the fight scene like a hurricane and into the news by predicting not only victory, but boldly declaring the very round he would knock out his opponent. His statements were unbelievably brash and bold.

He said things like: "I am the greatest of all times;" "If you even dream of beating me, you'd better wake up and apologize;" "Float like a butterfly, sting like a bee. Your hands can't hit what your eyes can't see;" "I'm so fast that last night I turned off the light switch in my hotel room and was in bed before the room was dark;" "I 'm so pretty. I'm pretty as a girl. I don't have a mark on my face; I'm a bad man! You must listen to me! I can't be beat! ... I'm the prettiest thing that ever lived!"

His statements were so outlandish he was called the "Louisville Lip." These were things you would never expect a man to say. But he was man enough to back up every word he spoke. His nemesis, Ken Norton, said, "Ali was a showman. He brought the eyes of the world toward boxing. But he could back up what he said."

He had grown up in the segregated south in Louisville, Kentucky. The pain of being treated like someone who was

Fight The Good Fight

inferior, subservient or even dirty had to have had an impact on his life.

Returning triumphantly from Rome to Louisville, Ali was bitterly disappointed at not being welcomed as an American hero in his segregated hometown. According to one story, after being refused service at a Louisville diner while wearing the Olympic medal around his neck, Ali threw it into the Ohio River."

He could be so charming, but in an instant he could turn cold and cruel. In a championship fight against Ernie Terrell in 1967 he kept yelling, "What's my name, fool? What's my name?" when Terrell insisted on calling him Cassius Clay.

He had the nerve to call the fearsome and ferocious Sonny Liston a "big ugly bear" and then had the courage to step into the boxing ring with the champion, who was considered unbeatable He outboxed, outmoved, outsmarted and outclassed the bigger, stronger, more powerful Liston, stopping him in the seventh round to win the heavyweight championship of the world at age 21. Nearly all of the writers and pundits had dismissed him as a loudmouth and a fake, and had picked Liston to win the fight.

Arthur Daley of the *New York Post* wrote before the fight, "The loudmouth from Louisville is likely to have a lot of vainglorious boasts jammed down his throat by a ham-like fist belonging to Liston, the malefic destroyer who is champion of the world."

After Clay's victory he shouted to reporters, "Eat your words! Eat your words! I am the greatest."

He belittled Joe Frazier and called him an "Uncle Tom." He also called him ugly. "Joe Frazier is so ugly he should donate his face to the U.S. Bureau of Wildlife."

This created a bitter rivalry with Frazier that he only was able to let go in recent years. "I don't think two big men ever fought fights like me and Joe Frazier," Ali said years later. "One fight maybe. But three times; we were the only ones. Of all the men I fought in boxing, Sonny Liston was the scariest; George Foreman was the most powerful; Floyd Patterson was the most skilled as a boxer, but the roughest and toughest was Joe Frazier. He brought out the best in me, and the best fight we fought was in Manila. So I'm sorry Joe Frazier is mad at me. I'm sorry I hurt him. Joe Frazier is a good man. I couldn't have done what I did without him, and he couldn't have done what he did without me."

Of George Foreman he said, "You think the world was shocked when Nixon resigned? Wait till I whup (sic) George Foreman's behind."

He angered and scared those whom he fought. He also angered and scared the establishment. "I am America. I am the part you won't recognize, but get used to me. Black, confident, cocky – my name, not yours. My religion, not yours. My goal, my own. Get used to me," Ali declared.

This was a time of social change in America. Rev. Martin Luther King led marches throughout the country fighting for equality. Naturally, black Americans wanted to stop discrimination and to be allowed the same opportunities as white Americans. There were race riots in most major cities and black power advocates who called for revolution.

"Slavery was over, but the black man felt suppressed. He felt that the whites wanted to keep him beneath him," said my good friend Warren Williams, a former professional heavyweight boxer from our gym.

"The black man has been emasculated," black activist Eldridge Cleaver said.

While Dr. Martin Luther King advocated non-violent protest, Malcolm X promoted active self -defense. "There can be no revolution without bloodshed," he said.

This was the culture that Muhammad Ali grew up in. He courageously stood up and shouted, "I'm black and I'm proud. I'm black and I'm pretty. Black is beautiful."

Fight The Good Fight

The white establishment didn't understand what caused this seething anger among blacks. I certainly didn't until I was older. My parents were the first generation off of the farm. They were blue-collar factory workers who lived paycheck to paycheck. I believe that most folks in our class, the lower middle class of America, felt that black folks were no worse off than the rest of us and had the same opportunities as everyone else in America. It wasn't until later in life that I realized how difficult it was for blacks in our country.

In the midst of this climate of racial tension came this incredible athlete, a big-mouthed, boxer who said whatever he felt no matter what. There were no euphemisms with Ali. He said what was on his mind and didn't care what anyone else thought. He was bold, blatant, conspicuous and loud. He courageously stood up against Sonny Liston, Joe Frazier, George Foreman, the establishment and the United States government, and won fights against every one of them.

"We idolized him because he said things that would have gotten us arrested if we had said them. He said things that black folks felt but didn't say publicly," said Williams.

"I loved Ali; I still do. As a young black, at times I was ashamed of my color; I was ashamed of my hair. And Ali made me proud. I'm just as happy being black now as you are being white, and Ali was a part of that growing process," said Baseball Hall of Fame member Reggie Jackson.

When we arrived at Navy Pier gym in Chicago that beautiful spring day to watch him train, there were about 100 other fans there to watch, too. After he trained and took a shower, he came out of the dressing room and walked onto the basketball floor of the gymnasium. He took a basketball and started shooting hook shots from half court, and was actually making some of the shots. As he did this the self-proclaimed greatest said, "I bet you Wilt Chamberlain can't do that."

Madison Square Garden boxing czar Harry Markson told of a similar experience: "I guess what I remember most about it wasn't the fight, but what happened after the weigh-in. Ali was walking across the floor of the arena. There was a basketball team practicing, and one of the players threw the ball to him. He was standing at mid-court, but he took a shot anyway, just flung the ball toward the basket. And I'll be if it didn't go in; swish. Everyone just stared in awe, but that was the kind of luck I figured followed Ali."

After he finished shooting baskets at Navy Pier that day, he entertained and mingled with the crowd. He signed autographs, kissed babies and hugged the young ladies. The adoring fans idolized the great boxing champion. The larger-than-life Ali had a soft side. He genuinely cared about people and loved to entertain.

Several months later during the week of Thanksgiving, I was in Cherry Hill, New Jersey with my wife Diane, her aunt Wanda and two cousins. Ali happened to live there. We went searching for his house. When we finally found it, there was Ali on the roof, gathering his own leaves. I hollered at him from the road above the house and he invited us into his driveway. I got out of the car and started talking with him. When he started down from the roof, I walked toward a ladder leaning on the house. My wife's cousins, Tracy and Todd Strachan, were about 11 and 12 years old. They began to challenge Ali to jump from the roof to which he replied an emphatic "No, no." Their challenges grew bolder and bolder as they continued to goad the champ by saying things like, "My grandmother's pump house is higher than that and I jump off of it all the time." No matter how much they teased him, Ali wouldn't jump, but opted to climb safely down the ladder.

When he came down from the roof, he started toward the front door of the house and said "Y'all come on in."

My wife and her aunt got out of the car and we all followed Ali into his beautiful house. He gave us a tour of the gorgeous home. I remember that it had a lovely courtyard in the center of the house and that he had an office in the basement where he autographed photos for each of us. I was curious why he was so good to us and ignorant enough to ask him. "Why are you being so nice to us?" I asked. "What do you mean?" he replied.

Kerry Pharr, left, and Todd and Tracy Strachan visit Muhammad Ali at his Cherry Hill, N.J. home in November 1971.

"Well, I always thought you hated white folks," I said. He was a little annoyed when he responded and said. "No! I don't hate white people."

Fight The Good Fight

This mean, cold-hearted boxing champion was really a teddy bear outside of the ring.

Champ, if you ever read this please forgive me for being so rude to ask you such a question after you had been so nice to us in your home.

Ali went on to reclaim his title by beating the young champion, George Foreman, in Zaire in the "Rumble in the Jungle." Just like they did years before when he fought Liston, everyone including some of those who trained him thought that Foreman would kill him. But Ali man-handled the great undefeated young champion with his unique "rope-a-dope" style. He lay on the ropes and allowed Foreman to tire himself out. He became the most recognizable face in the world, adored everywhere and welcomed into the homes of movie stars and kings alike. Even Elvis Presley gave him a boxing robe reported to cost $5,000. He became so famous that when he spoke, E.F. Hutton listened. I was in the New Orleans Superdome on September 15, 1978, when Ali regained his title for the third time from Leon Spinks, the young man who had won the 1976 Olympic gold medal in Montreal in the light-heavyweight division. Spinks had out-hustled the aging Ali to win his championship several months before. The Superdome was filled with 63,350 people to see Ali win his title back. Ali had the ability to draw crowds normally reserved for the Super Bowl. While there that night, I could tell Ali's skills had greatly diminished and even though he won I knew the end of his career was near.

He fought two more times and lost both bouts. He fought champion Larry Holmes on October 2, 1980, and was stopped in the 10th round. Then on December 12, 1981, he faced future world champion Trevor Berbick and lost a 10-round unanimous decision. Because of his diminished skills, he took a lot of punishment in both of those bouts which were very hard on his body.

Fight The Good Fight

Since retiring from the ring, Ali suffers from Parkinson's disease, a neurological affliction that causes tremors, loss of balance, memory lapses and confusion. Doctors believe Ali's disease was caused by repeated blows to the head that he suffered in the latter part of his career. Many believe his last two bouts were the worst on his body. The young Ali was almost untouchable, but late in his career he would lay on the boxing ropes in his "rope a dope" style. I believe it was the stigma of slavery, the continued oppression, prejudice, inequality and hatred toward blacks that created this anger in Ali and black America. Slavery was wrong and it was evil. Jesus, the God-man who gave us the greatest gift of all when he voluntarily laid down his life so that others might live said, *"By this all will know that you are my disciples, if you have love one for another."* (John 13:35.)

Children in Sunday school sing a song called, "Jesus loves the little children, all the children of the world, red and yellow, black and white; they are **all** precious in his sight."

Jesus gave us a commission and said, *"Go into all the world and preach the gospel to ever creature."* (Mark 16:15.)

We have a responsibility to love all and to tell all about the love of Jesus. *"Beloved let us love one another for love is of God; and everyone who loves is born of God and knows God. He who does not love does not know God, for God is love."* (1 John 4:7.)

When I managed the career of junior welterweight Continental of Americas champion Darryl "Fast Fists" Fuller, we became so close that Fuller, who is African-American often would say to me, "Kerry, you know how them white people do you." I'd laughingly reply, "Yeah, Darryl, I know how they do you." But prejudice and hatred aren't a white thing or a black thing; they are an individual thing. Each of us chooses in his heart to love or hate our fellow man. In reality, all of us are sinners regardless of our race or ethnicity. The

Bible declares that God made all of us from one blood and we are equal in God's eyes (Acts 17:26).

At a time when times were really tough for blacks in America, Ali stood up defiantly and spoke out about the things he thought were wrong. He gave pride to black America and he gave them a voice that could be heard. He was a heroic icon for black people and black pride. To the rest of us he was simply "The Greatest." Ironically, the former hated Black Muslim has become a cultural icon for the world.

Big John Tate

When I was in my 30s, I opened a boxing gym to work with the youth in Middle Tennessee. I was a professional boxing manager and trainer, and was managing heavyweight boxer Keith McKnight. I had been developing him since he was a teenager. We had been working together for about nine years. We had traveled many miles together during his amateur and professional careers. He was a hot boxing prospect

His professional record was very impressive: 33 wins with only one loss. McKnight was on a roll and had won four consecutive bouts. His next fight was scheduled on national television on USA's Tuesday Night Fights against the rugged Obed Sullivan, the No. 4- rated heavyweight boxer in the world.

While we were training for the fight at Horace Kent's gym in Knoxville, Tennessee, Big John Tate, the former heavyweight champion of the world, walked into the gym. I had known Tate for almost 20 years. Ace Miller brilliantly had managed Tate's career and developed him into the heavy-weight world champion. He had earned about $2 million in boxing, but had squandered it all on drug abuse and petty crime. He had lost his money, house and cars. Even worse, he lost his wife, and his reputation was in shreds.

John found out that McKnight had a big fight coming up on television, and he asked if he could help prepare McKnight for the Sullivan bout. McKnight and I took a chance on John, and we took him back to our home in the Middle Tennessee area. John stayed in a little apartment in the back of the gym for several weeks before the fight. Most people lock their doors at night before they lay down to sleep. Not Big John; he slept soundly right next to a door standing wide open all night long.

Fight The Good Fight

Several people who knew John's history asked questions like, "Why do you have that crack head working with you?"

I personally saw it as an opportunity for the former heavyweight champion of the world to give McKnight some insight on how to win the fight with Sullivan. I also saw it as an opportunity to help John get his life back on track.

Often someone would recognize Tate and ask, "Aren't you Big John Tate, the former heavyweight champion of the world?"

John would reply, "Yeah! I was the baddest man on the planet for a minute."

A couple of days before the fight, our team flew to the boxing venue in Connecticut for the weigh-in and pre-fight physicals. After the bout, with Sullivan we returned to the Nashville airport where my car was parked. John was not scheduled to leave for Knoxville for several hours so he asked me to drop him off in downtown Nashville.

John asked me to let him out at the housing projects on Lafayette Street. I asked him if he was sure, and he said yes. I was saddened because I thought he was going there to buy drugs. We said goodbye, and I never saw the champ again.

Six weeks later, Big John was driving a pick-up truck when a brain tumor compressed an artery at the base of his skull. The truck slammed into a telephone pole, killing him almost instantly at age 43.

Speaking of George

For all his great accomplishments and fortunes achieved in and outside the ring, the fearsome George Foreman's greatest triumph was his acceptance of Jesus Christ. In his youth, Foreman was described as a sullen brute that would beat someone up as opposed to help them. In the early days of his career, he carried this anger into the ring with him and was very vicious and mean in the ring. I remember seeing him push some of his own cornermen around the ring after they had angered him.

He stormed through the heavyweight division, devastating great fighters such as Joe Frazier and Ken Norton. However, he suffered an ignominious defeat in Zaire, Africa, to the incomparable Muhammad Ali. Foreman resumed his career, seeking a rematch but Ali wisely didn't fight a return bout. Something happened to Foreman after losing a decision to fellow contender Jimmy Young in 1977. Foreman ended up lying prostrate on the floor in his dressing room and had what may be best described as a near- death experience. During this experience, he says he saw a vision of people trapped in hell and a vision of Jesus Christ. This is how Foreman described part of that experience and his conversion to Jesus Christ as told to David Mainse on the television program *100 Huntley Street:*

"I had just fought a fight with Jimmy Young...just a decision, it wasn't a tough fight or anything. After I found out I had lost, I went back to the dressing room ... just a normal cooling off. And let me tell you business picked up for me there! I had always prayed to God. I believed there was probably a God somewhere; and I'd always said, 'No matter what, everybody got their own religion as long as they treat people right it's OK.' But when I left that dressing room, I was screaming the name of Jesus. I started screaming words like 'hallelujah I've been born again.' They thought I was crazy and hurt, so they took me to the hospital. They thought I was losing my mind. And they ran all kinda tests on me for two or three days, and nothin' was wrong with me. But I saw the glory of God...I saw it! And let me tell you that Jesus is alive ... there's a living God, and I didn't even know it. I was wondering about it before, but now I'm not wondering. I know! And I thank God because there are a lot of people who think for sure ... and some think maybe, or maybe not. But I know. God ... I don't know ... for some reason touched me, an old sinner. There are a lot of clean men out in the world doing everything right, and He showed me that there's a living God.

George Foreman retired from boxing after that fight and became a preacher. In the late 1980s, he returned to boxing. Many people laughed at Big George when he returned, given his advanced age and heavy weight. But, George kept winning fights. He landed a title shot against Evander Holyfield and acquitted himself well in losing a 12-round decision. Many thought George should hang it up after that fight.

But, George and his faith persevered. He continued to fight and eventually landed another title shot against champion Michael Moorer. For 10 rounds, Moorer boxed circles around Foreman. The television announcers (Foreman's colleagues at HBO) were talking about how badly Foreman was losing. However, Foreman landed one big chopping right hand and KO'd the champ. Announcer Jim Lampley exclaimed, "My God, he's done it." Foreman became the oldest heavyweight champion in history at the ripe old age of 45. Foreman persevered and triumphed because of his faith in the Lord.

Knocked Down In the First Round

Darryl "Fast Fists" Fuller was a world class junior welterweight boxer who I co-trained and managed. In March of 1985 I was instrumental in landing Fuller a fight for the World Boxing Council's Continental of Americas junior welterweight championship.

Kel "Special K" Robin was the reigning champion. Robin was 6-foot, which was tall for a 140-pound fighter. He was an excellent boxer/puncher from Miami. Marty Cohen, also from Miami and president of the WBC's Continental of America's Championship Committee, was helping develop Robin.

Robin was promoted by Don King Productions. So in order to secure the fight for Fuller we had to sign a promotional agreement with the one and only Don King. We had about six weeks to get Fuller ready for the bout, and Darryl trained very hard.

Darryl was a seasoned veteran with an outstanding amateur background. He was a vicious and fearless fighter, 5-foot-7, with a powerful, muscular body. His fighting style was one of aggression and constant pressure. He would get very close to his opponent, throw a tremendous number of punches and make his opponent fight instead of allowing them to box. Fuller's style never allowed his opponents to rest.

He had a habit of grunting or barking every time he threw a punch. This was very unnerving for his opponent. This constant pressure usually wore his opponents down emotionally and physically. Fuller often talked about how long it would take him to break another fighter down, or how many rounds he would need to take his opponent's heart. Fuller waged a war of attrition against his opponents, and it usually took him several rounds to take them apart.

Fight The Good Fight

Darryl was all business in the ring whether sparring at the gym or in a fight. He was vicious in sparring sessions and fights alike. He wasn't the type of fighter that you could ask to take it easy on an inexperienced boxer. Because of his style, he would hurt boxers like that. If you climbed into the ring with him you needed to be ready and able to fight or you had no business in the ring with him.

Darryl and I did a lot of things together outside of the ring. He had never spent much time in the country so I often took him to rural places in the mountains along with some of the other fighters. We went to ride out falls in Alabama and Fall Creek Falls State Resort Park in Tennessee. Fall Creek Falls boasts the highest waterfall in the United States east of the Mississippi River.

One of the funniest things I remember about Darryl was seeing an opossum in the middle of the road as we were driving on one of our rural trips. Darryl began hollering, "Run over that possum, Kerry!" "Man you're crazy I'm not running over that possum," I laughingly replied, "Yeah, run over it," he hollered. "No! I'm not running over that possum with my car," I said. After we had passed the animal without hitting it, Darryl looked at me and sadly said, "Man, that's the best tasting sandwich meat there is – especially when you put some hot sauce on it."

The fight with Robin was at the Las Vegas Rivera Hotel. As we were entering the ring for the title bout, I noticed comedian and television star Redd Foxx sitting ringside in our corner. He was talking to former welterweight world champion Hedgeman Lewis. I focused my attention on Fuller, listening to the ring announcer introduce him and the current champion Robin.

After the introductions, referee Davey Pearl called us to the center of the ring and we listened to his instructions. We returned to our corner and I helped Fuller take off his robe while Rev. Leroy Ozier, his co-trainer, quickly inserted his mouthpiece. Just then, the timekeeper rang the bell and the fight began.

Rev. Leroy Ozier, left, Darryl "Fast Fists" Fuller and Kerry Pharr visit before Fuller's championship fight vs. Gary Hinton in Atlantic City, N.J.

Uncharacteristically, Fuller walked straight at his much taller opponent with his left hand down. Robin seized this golden opportunity by throwing a perfectly timed, straight, fast-and-hard right hand that landed flush on Fuller's chin. Darryl went down like he had hit a tree limb while riding a motorcycle, only 15 seconds after the fight had started.

Bobby Goodman, vice president of boxing for Don King Productions, told me after the bout that he thought Fuller was about to get blown out of the fight in the first round and stink up his televised boxing card. Everyone in the auditorium thought the fight had ended and that Robin had destroyed Fuller.

However, Fuller slowly and calmly rose to his feet at the count of eight. He looked at Reverend Ozier and me in his corner. Both of us were frantically hollering instructions to him. He nodded as if to say, *I'm OK and I know what to do*. The referee wiped Darryl's gloves and motioned for the boxers to continue fighting.

In preparation for this bout, we had traveled to Morristown, Tennessee, where Darryl sparred with future world champion Frankie "The Surgeon" Randall. Randall was a great fighter and would later be the first fighter to beat and dethrone the great junior welterweight champion Julio Cesar Chavez. When we were there, Randall and Fuller tried to kill each other. One day Fuller got the best of Randall; the next day, Randall got the best of Fuller. Back and forth they went at each other. Fuller had trained extremely hard for this fight and he had sparred with a future hall of fame fighter. He was in incredible shape and ready for whatever Robin could deliver.

Robin tried his best to crush Fuller, but he wasn't able to land another clean shot, and he couldn't discourage Darryl. As Darryl returned to the corner at the end of the first round, Rev. Ozier and I tried to remain calm and to let Darryl know that he was OK and that he could still win the bout.

Fuller was as cool as a butcher working in a freezer. Remember Rocky Balboa hammering those carcasses in the icy freezer. Fuller had the same sort of determination as the fictional Balboa made so famous by Sylvester Stallone.

From the second round forward, Fuller began to impose his will on Robin. He drew Robin into a brawl and began to rough the champion up and slowly break him down. The war of attrition and the war of wills played out during the next seven brutal rounds. Fuller and Robin were battering each

Fight The Good Fight

other like two rock-em, sock-em robots. I could see Robin slowly coming apart.

The constant pressure Fuller applied finally broke Robin down physically and emotionally. Fuller devastatingly knocked Robin down for the first time in the ninth round, again in the 10th and two more times in the 11th. Fortunately, Davey Pearl stepped in and stopped the fight before Fuller hurt Robin even more. Fuller won the bout and the championship via a technical knockout in the 11th round. I was excited my fighter had won, but I felt very sorry for Kel Robin, who was now a broken and defeated man. I never heard of him again. Fuller had effectively ended his career that night on March 15, 1985. Darryl Fuller became a champion because he had the strength and courage to get up and fight another round. He survived the adversity early in the first round to overcome the odds and become a champion. Perhaps he drew on the wisdom of Solomon from Proverbs 3:5-6.

Fight The Good Fight

Darryl "Fast Fists" Fuller wears his Continental of Americas championship belt.

Mark Gastineau... Pro Football's King of Sack

Mark Gastineau is a former all-pro defensive end in the National Football League who played for the New York Jets from 1979 until '88. A ferocious pass rusher, he accumulated 100.5 quarterback sacks in his first 100 starts in the league. In 1984, Gastineau set the record for most sacks in a single season (22), which stood for 16 years until the New York Giants' Michael Strahan controversially broke it in 2001, as Green Bay quarterback Brett Favre seemingly allowed Strahan to sack him.

Gastineau retired from professional football and began a career in professional boxing. Those who managed his boxing career wanted to capitalize on his name and build an impressive record for him against hand-picked opponents. Their goal was to secure a huge payday against former heavyweight champion George Foreman. Because of his sheer size, brute strength and athletic ability, Mark would have won some professional boxing matches against the right opponents without any training.

However those around him used him as a pawn and led him to believe he was actually a good boxer. I'm confident he was unaware of the lengths his manager and trainer would sink to in order to secure a huge payday for the well-known football player. Two years after he began his boxing career I unwittingly would become involved in a fixed fight featuring Gastineau.

In the spring of 1993, former heavyweight boxing contender /character actor Randall "Tex" Cobb who lived in Nashville at the time, started training at Club Knockout, a boxing gym that I managed. This was the home of our amateur boxing team and my professional boxers. In the next few months, the boxers and I got to know the personable Cobb fairly well. Cobb had been retired from boxing for several years, but was on the comeback trail. He had strung together

Fight The Good Fight

several wins and was attempting to fight his way back into contention to become heavyweight world champion.

In his first career as a boxer, Cobb served as the proverbial punching bag for heavyweight champion Larry Holmes in a fight so one-sided that ringside announcer Howard Cosell decided to call it quits as a boxing announcer. Cosell supposedly was outraged the noncompetitive fight was allowed to continue. Larry Holmes was one of the greatest heavyweight boxers I've ever seen and his left jab might have even been better than Muhammad Ali's. It was almost impossible for other boxers to get past his jab. He made nearly all his opponents look ordinary.

Although Cobb wasn't blessed with great skills, he was unbelievably tough and durable. He took everything Holmes dished out that night and never buckled or went down. I don't believe there was an opportunity for the referee to stop the bout in spite of the Cosell criticism.

At the end of Cobb's first boxing career, I was in the building and saw with my own eyes he and former heavyweight champion Leon Spinks nearly beat each other to death in a match Cobb won at Municipal Auditorium in Nashville. Cobb was definitely a rock-'em, sock-'em type of fighter. In his prime, he was also one of the toughest men ever to lace on a pair of gloves.

While training with us at Club Knockout, Cobb indicated he wanted to fight again in a main event in Nashville. He told me his manager, "Elvis" Rick Parker, who also managed heavyweight contender "Smokin" Bert Cooper and Gastineau, wanted to promote in Nashville. He said Parker didn't have a license in the state and needed a local promoter to co-promote the show. I'd read somewhere that Parker wasn't the most honest guy, but I had never met Rick and didn't know anything about him other than I occasionally would see him in the corner with Gastineau and Cooper in bouts on television.

Fight The Good Fight

Through the years, I had worked with many other promoters even the one and only Don King without incident. In fact, Bob Goodman, the vice president of boxing at Don King Productions, asked me to help him get officials for a world championship fight they were doing in Nashville. I'd met Bobby years before and Bobby is a great guy. So I introduced him to several local officials who were hired as judges, referees, physicians and even a timekeeper for the event.

Even though I was somewhat leery of working with Parker I was enamored with the thought of being involved with a promotion involving famous boxers Cobb, Cooper and Gastineau. Tex Cobb was famous for his involvement in boxing and for his biker role in the Nicolas Cage movie *Raising Arizona*. I felt that he would draw a very large crowd to the auditorium and it would be a profitable promotion.

During a conversation with Cobb, I explained my concerns about working with Parker. He told me he would fight in the main event and that we should do well at the gate. As for Parker, he said to make sure you protect yourself. So I spoke with Parker on the phone and we verbally agreed to do the show together. We were to use my promoter's license. In essence, I was a front man for Parker who was the actual promoter. In exchange for the use of my license, Parker would put Tex Cobb in the main event, and place Bert Cooper in an exhibition against five different boxers. Parker also said he would give Mark Gastineau and my fighter Keith McKnight undercard bouts. We agreed to a 50-50 split of the profit from the event.

Ken "The Bull" Atkin, left, Randall "Tex Cobb and Kerry Pharr at the Club Knockout Gym.

During the next six weeks or so, I worked very hard to help promote the show that was to showcase Cobb in the main event. Cobb continued to come to our gym and to spar with our boxers. Everyone was working hard for the upcoming summer show. I had posters printed, we did press conferences, radio and television interviews to promote the upcoming event. Everything was going well and ticket sales were brisk. The local fans were excited and it looked like the event was going to be a huge success. Then, about a week before the show, Cobb mysteriously pulled out of the fight even though he was healthy and hadn't been injured while training. I thought it was bizarre and it really perplexed me. Why was Cobb pulling out of the fight? For the life of me, I didn't understand it.

I'd invested so much time and money in the show and was worried I might take a financial beating on the promotion. Parker assured me everything would be OK and that we should move forward with the event. Travel and lodging arrangements had been made for the participants on the show so I agreed to carry on as planned.

A couple of days later, the 300-hundred pound Parker and his entourage arrived. Cooper and Gastineau flew into town with their respective trainers. Parker drove to the gym in a two-seat white Mercedes with a girl from a local escort service by his side.

Kenny Merritt, one of the heavyweights in our gym, sparred with the dangerous Bert Cooper. Gastineau's trainer held the hand mitts and had him hit those but he didn't allow him to spar with anyone. While watching him train it was evident to everyone in the gym that Mark was a novice boxer. A couple of local pro's working out in the gym said to me almost in unison, "Kerry, please get me a fight with him." Mark had a big name and these guys wanted to add it to their boxing resume.

I felt sorry for Gastineau because I could see he couldn't box and I was certain that his handlers were only using him to land a payday. They weren't investing the necessary time to build boxing skills.

During those few days Gastineau was in our gym, I got to talk to him one-on-one quite a bit and I really liked him. He had gone through some hard times and had been in a lot of trouble. He told me he had given his life to Christ and was trying to follow Him. I could see he was having some challenges in his walk as a Christian. I remembered how difficult it had been for me, in those early years as a Christian and

Fight The Good Fight

the slow process of growth I went through. I reflected on my many failures as a believer in Christ and I could tell it was not easy for Mark either. I was saddened to see what he was going through and how his management team used him for its own purposes.

The event was scheduled for Saturday June 18, 1993, at Nashville's Municipal Auditorium. Parker privately had arranged for a boxing manager from South Carolina to bring an opponent for Gastineau. Terry Miller was the fighter's name and his boxing record was 0 wins and 10 losses. Gastineau's record that night was 14-1 against handpicked opposition.

The crowd roared in excitement as the match began. The smaller Miller was quicker than Gastineau. Miller began hitting Mark with quick, clean punches as he darted in and out while the confused Gastineau swatted at but missed his elusive opponent. Miller easily won the first and second rounds and was handily winning the third round. Gastineau looked like he didn't have a clue about what was going on and why he couldn't hit his opponent. It was evident Mark was losing the fight. The crowd was cheering for him and imploring him to fight. Suddenly, without a punch being thrown, Miller abruptly fell down and didn't get up. I've seen fighters lay down before in venues all across America. But it usually was because they were overmatched, scared, taking a beating or completely exhausted, and they didn't want to get seriously hurt. However, this was shockingly overt since Miller hadn't been hurt and was sailing to an easy victory. The referee stood above him and counted to 10. Gastineau was credited with another knockout on his record. The auditorium crowd smelled a rat and began harmoniously chanting "bull , bull , bull ."

After the show ended, Parker and I met with Bob Skoney the auditorium manager. Skoney paid Parker for the ticket sales at the gate that night. Parker then paid the remaining

Fight The Good Fight

bills and the fighters out of the proceeds. He looked at me and said, "You and I will settle up later." I replied, "OK, that's fine." He then stuck the balance of $15,000 into his briefcase. I never saw, heard from or talked to Parker again. But I didn't care. The thing that was much, much worse to me than not getting my share of the gate was that I had badly tarnished my reputation by being involved with Parker and the promotion. That hurt me more than anything.

On October 4, 1993, *Sports Illustrated* published an article titled "The Fix Was In." The article accused Rick Parker of traveling around the country with Tex Cobb and Mark Gastineau and fixing fights in their favor. Although there was no concrete proof of wrongdoing by these guys, suddenly it all made sense to me and I understood why Cobb had pulled out of the fight. In fact, Cobb later won a huge lawsuit that subsequently was overturned on appeal against *Sports Illustrated* for harming his reputation.

Gastineau knew he wasn't fighting the toughest guy in the world, but I honestly didn't believe he knew Parker was paying his opponent to lay down that night. However, the *Sports Illustrated* article reported that he was aware of what was going on in his fights.

Things did not end well for Rick Parker. On April 28, 1995, Tim "Doc" Anderson a professional boxer that Parker had formerly managed and allegedly poisoned before a boxing match against Gastineau, confronted Parker in a Florida hotel room. Anderson said an argument ensued as Parker began yelling and cursing at him, including making threatening comments about his disabled sister Erin. Anderson pulled a pistol from his pocket and shot Parker to death.

The trouble between Parker and Anderson had started several years before in 1990. Parker originally was Anderson's boxing manger until he picked up Gastineau and Cooper. According to Anderson, Parker had stolen his earnings from boxing matches on the pretense of putting it in an escrow account for him. Reportedly Parker had spent $150,000 of Anderson's money on cocaine.

As noted earlier Parker began building Gastineau in anticipation of a huge payday against George Foreman, but Gastineau was having trouble beating the opponents that Parker was handpicking for him. After Gastineau had won nine professional fights, Parker secured a fight for him on USA's Tuesday Night Fights. He needed a safe opponent for Gastineau and he allegedly offered Anderson $500,000 to lose to Gastineau on television June 6, 1992. Anderson refused and gave Gastineau a beating that night.

To get Gastineau back on track, Parker needed a win over Anderson. He talked Anderson into a rematch and again asked him to take a dive but Anderson again refused. Anderson and Gastineau fought again in Oklahoma City, Oklahoma, on December 3, 1992 where Parker supposedly paid a corner man in Anderson's corner to place poison in Anderson's drinking water. Anderson became very ill during the fight and was knocked out by Gastineau in the sixth round. The effects of the drugs never wore off. Anderson was sick and bed-ridden for much of the next couple of years. He constantly was vomiting and would bump into walls while walking and fall down.

Parker then reportedly had Anderson beaten with a baseball bat by two masked thugs who also threatened to kill his sister and her two children if he didn't stop the allegations about his poisoning and Parker's fight fixing. Anderson's sister had been paralyzed in a diving accident and when the goon's told him that Parker knew his sister's address he took it as a personal threat against her and that was the thing that drove him to meet with Parker.

Anderson said he took a pistol with him because Parker was known to carry a gun and he was afraid to meet him without a weapon. I've never met Anderson but everything that I've read or heard about him is that he is a decent guy who only wanted to protect himself, his sister and her children. His biggest mistake in life was to have been associated with Parker.

Steven Canton wrote an article about Anderson titled, "The Story of an Unfair Trial." In it he said – "Tim "Doc" Anderson was convicted of a crime he did not commit. He was found guilty of premeditated first-degree murder and has been incarnated since April 1995 in a Florida prison, serving life with no chance for parole. Yes, Tim Anderson did shoot and kill his former promoter on that fateful day, but it definitely was not premeditated. If he had been convicted of anything less, he would have already served his time and been a free man."

I've made many mistakes in my life by being involved with people that I shouldn't have been with. Fortunately, we never attempted to kill anyone. Sadly though, there were times in my life when I was a bad influence on others. I encouraged others to do wrong. Thankfully, the Lord protected me during those sinful years. I wish I could go back and correct those things. I wish that I could take back the hurt that I've caused others. But I can't. All I can do is learn from my past mistakes and to be loving, gentle and kind to those who cross my path today and every day that I have left.

The Bible teaches Christians not to be unequally yoked together with unbelievers (2 Corinthians 6:14). In this scripture the Bible asks the question: *"What does righteousness and wickedness have in common?"* The answer is nothing. Those who are wicked will do evil things and although those who are righteous will try to avoid them they will be a party to the evil because they are unnaturally yoked or partnered together with the unbeliever.

After I became a Christian, I shouldn't have partnered with unbelievers. There's nothing wrong with helping someone who doesn't share your belief or value system, if you aren't helping them to do evil. However, if you are a

Fight The Good Fight

partner with someone who is an unrighteous person and they do something unethical, illegal or even wicked it will reflect badly on you as well, even though you may be totally innocent. People who don't share your belief system always will try to get you to compromise your standards.

My dreams and aspirations clouded my judgment and like a fool I rushed right into numerous bad situations. Fortunately, the Lord protected me from danger and led me down a righteous path – a path that I strive constantly to follow to the best of my ability.

A Tribute to Luther Burgess

Almost every boxing fan has heard of the legendary boxing trainer Eddie Futch, who trained 21 world champions, including five heavyweight champions. But many fans do not recognize the name Luther Burgess. Luther, who fought as a featherweight from 1946 to 1949, was Eddie's first professional boxer. Back in the summer of 1997, Luther talked with me about his early life in boxing. At the time, neither of us had a clue that tragedy would strike both of us with a sorrow beyond words shortly thereafter. Luther began reminiscing by telling me about the fateful day future hall of fame trainer Eddie Futch spotted him as a teenager playing baseball. Luther said Eddie shouted out, "Hey kid, when you get through playin', come see me and I'll teach you how to box."

Luther went on to explain, "There was something about the way he said what he said that really got to me."

Luther mused, "You know, you can play basketball, you can play football, and you can play baseball, but you can't play boxing."

Luther eventually gave up baseball and allowed Eddie to mold him into a pretty good professional boxer. When Luther learned the sport of boxing, fighters weren't protected; so when an opportunity came along to make some money, they took it. In Luther's eighth, ninth and 10th professional fights, he faced a top featherweight contender and two future hall-of-fame world champions. Amazingly, all of these fights occurred within a span of just four months. On April 4th, 1948, Luther faced top featherweight contender Jock Leslie, who he defeated in a 10-round decision. Two months later on June 25th, Luther faced the great featherweight world champion Willie "Will o' the Wisp" Pep, whose record at the time was an astonishing 126-1. Here was young Luther Burgess challenging one of the greatest feath-

Fight The Good Fight

erweight champions of all time in only his ninth professional fight. Even so, Luther went the distance, losing a 10-round decision with the future hall of fame champion.

Then, only one month later, Luther Burgess and Eddie Futch arrived in New Orleans on the train from Detroit to face future lightweight champion Joe "Old Bones" Brown. This fight saw Luther go the distance yet again, with Luther managing a respectable draw with the future world champion. Luther fought five more times before retiring from boxing in 1949. When he retired, Luther became – as you might have guessed – a boxing trainer. Those who knew him well say Luther could have become as famous as Eddie Futch and Emanuel Steward if it were not for some unfortunate personal problems. In fact, those who worked the closest with Luther will argue that Luther was a truly outstanding trainer. While working for Steward at the famous Kronk Gym in Detroit for many years, Luther contributed greatly to the impressive Kronk legacy of many well-trained and highly accomplished boxers. About this same period in 1997 when Luther shared details about his early career in boxing, I was managing and training Keith McKnight. Keith was a very quick, mobile heavy-weight. I felt that Keith needed a great trainer to take him to the next level. I was sure that if we could help him improve just a little, we might actually get a shot at the heavyweight championship. Since Emanuel Steward was training Lennox Lewis at the time, I didn't think we would have much of a chance getting Emanuel to work with Keith. However, I had become friends with Luther and I decided to ask for his help.

When I first approached Luther by phone about training McKnight, he turned us down. So Keith and I got on a plane and flew from Nashville to Detroit to talk face-to-face with Luther. We immediately went to his house and asked Luther to ride with us to Grand Rapids, Michigan, to watch Keith spar with Buster Mathis Jr., During the sparring session that day, Keith looked sensational against Buster, which impressed

Luther so much that he indicated he might be willing to work with us after all. However, since Luther was still employed by Emanuel Steward at Kronk Gym, and because Steward always had been very good to him, Luther told us he had to make sure Emanuel would support his decision before making the commitment to train McKnight.

Longtime trainer Luther Burgess of Detroit's Kronk Gym finds himself surrounded by Adam Richards, left, Keith McKnight, Kerry Pharr and Mark Frazee.

We arranged to have lunch with the personable Emanuel so that Luther would have an opportunity to request permission to help McKnight with his career. During the meeting, Emanuel gladly gave his blessing, saying he was very happy for Luther to have a chance to make some money. In fact, Emanuel allowed McKnight to train at the Kronk Gym for his first fight with Luther as his trainer.

Keith won that first fight in a unanimous 10-round

Fight The Good Fight

decision against Ed Donaldson on May 1, 1997, in Asbury Park, New Jersey. HBO commentator Harold Lederman made several flattering comments about McKnight's great corner with Luther Burgess as the chief second. For McKnight's second fight with Luther as his trainer, we held our training camp at the Roy Jones Gym in Pensacola, Florida. Former cruiserweight world champion Al Cole was one of Roy's fighters. At the time, Al was at the gym preparing for an upcoming bout himself. Roy's company, Square Ring, and Coach Alton Merkerson graciously provided us with a place to stay and the opportunity for terrific sparring sessions with Cole.

After we broke training camp in Pensacola, we traveled to our home base in Nashville. Since Luther grew up in the South, he really enjoyed southern-style cooking, so we went all out in an attempt to show him our best southern hospitality. We made sure he got all of his favorite southern foods like gravy and biscuits, country ham, fried chicken, catfish, chocolate pie and banana pudding. Luther seemed to have a wonderful time in Nashville; I still can picture him stretched out in a lounge chair in my back yard under a shade tree while taking a nap following an enjoyable meal at my house.

After our brief stay in Nashville, we flew to Lewiston, Idaho, where Keith would face Bryan Scott in the 10-round main event of a Cedric Kushner Productions show, which was staged on the nearby Nez Perce Indian reservation. In this second fight under Luther's tutelage, Keith made short work of Scott by stopping him in the first round. Luther had prepared Keith well for both fights; and the future looked very rosy for Team McKnight. After the fight, Luther flew home to Detroit. The next day, according to Luther's wife, Luther went out to celebrate the win. The very next morning, the 70-year old trainer suffered a stroke that paralyzed him and left him unable to speak. In September, my first wife Diane and I flew to Detroit to see

Luther in the hospital. During the visit, we prayed with him and spent time telling Luther how much we cared for him. Sadly, a few days after we returned to Nashville, Diane was diagnosed with breast cancer. Luther lived only a few months more, and my precious wife Diane passed away four years later.

Having had the opportunity to know and work with Luther Burgess represents an enormous blessing in my life. Luther was a great father, great husband and a great boxing trainer. He also was a good friend. Rest in peace, Luther.

Diamond Jim MacDonald

We had just landed in Johannesburg, South Africa, from a very long and tiring flight. I was with Diamond Jim MacDonald, a professional boxer who was scheduled to box Thulane "Sugar Boy" Malinga, a fighter who later would become a world champion, in the main event of a boxing show. MacDonald and I left the United States two days before our arrival in South Africa. We flew from Kennedy International Airport in New York to London's Heathrow International Airport, where we had a 14-hour layover.

Besides being a light-heavyweight contender, MacDonald, was an avid antique collector and dealer. We touched down in London just after daybreak and weren't scheduled to leave for South Africa until that night, so we took the train downtown.

We got off of the train in the heart of the city at Piccadilly Circus. After breakfast MacDonald wanted to hunt for antiques, so we spent most of the day in and out of antique shops along the Thames River. Near the end of the day MacDonald found an antique bottle he really liked that had been fished out of the Thames. He purchased it and we made our way back to Heathrow for our evening departure.

We were flying South African Airlines. This was during the days of Apartheid – a sordid system of racial separation – and the airline had a policy of searching every passenger and their baggage before boarding. The plane was very slow in boarding because of the policy.

Many countries were boycotting the white-ruled South African government because of their segregation policies. Therefore, South African Airlines wasn't permitted to fly the shortest route down the continent of Africa; instead, the plane was forced to fly the much longer route around the Ivory Coast. We flew for seven hours and landed on a small Island west of the Ivory Coast to refuel the giant 747 jet. Once

Fight The Good Fight

refueled, the plane took off immediately and after another arduous seven hours of flying we landed in Johannesburg, the capital of South Africa.

As we made our way through customs, the promoters of the show, South African Thinus Strydom and Ireland native Jim Harvey, greeted us. On the way to the baggage claim area Strydom and Harvey tried to make us feel comfortable and welcomed us to their country. We picked up our baggage and went outside to a waiting car that was to take us to our hotel in Johannesburg, or Jo-burg, as the natives call it.

After we placed our luggage in the trunk of the vehicle we were introduced to a black native South African driver. Immediately he turned around and said to me in English, "So Kerry, what do you think of Jimmy Swaggart and his trouble with the prostitute?"

Since I was a Christian, I was in shock that someone on the other side of the world, from another culture, would know or care about something that happened with the most popular television preacher in the United States.

Swaggart, had apologized on national television in America for being photographed entering a seedy motel outside of New Orleans with a known prostitute just before MacDonald and I departed for Africa. I thought, "Wow, our influence for good or bad sure travels a long way."

I instantly felt guilty for the times I had failed the Lord and had been a bad influence for others. I remembered times when my testimony had been destroyed because of my own sin.

Jimmy Swaggart was born and raised in Ferriday, Louisiana. His first cousins were Jerry Lee Lewis, an early rock and roll legend, and Mickey Gilley, a country music recording artist. All three of them were very gifted musically and grew up playing the piano and singing. Lewis and Gilley achieved fame and fortune in the music business. Swaggart went into the ministry as an Assembly of God preacher. Early

Fight The Good Fight

in his career, he began broadcasting his sermons on the radio. Later, he began preaching on television and some 10 years later, 200 stations carried the Jimmy Swaggart telecast into 2 million households. He was highly regarded and respected in the United States. His church had a membership of 4,000 and he had started a Christian college that was thriving.

Sadly, Jimmy Swaggart and Jim Bakker, another television minister, both had been caught in immoral situations with women they weren't married to, within one year of each other. This hurt many people all around the world and the cause of Christ as well. Both Swaggart and Bakker's ministries were, by and large, finished. Although both repented of their sins and resumed TV ministries, neither of them has regained the prominence or stature they once held.

I tried to explain to our South African driver what Swaggart did was terribly wrong and that each of us has a sinful nature and is prone to do wicked things even after we become Christians. I explained to him we all have a sinful nature or a natural propensity to sin and any person was capable of falling into grievous sin just as Swaggart had. The Bible tells us that *"There is none righteous, no, not one."* (Romans 3:10).

Dr. Jack Graham, pastor of the great Prestonwood Baptist Church of Plano, Texas, recently commented on the failure of Christian leaders at a service I attended there. "It's not the efficiency of the messenger, but the sufficiency of the scripture," he said. What Dr. Graham was saying is that it's the word of God that changes men's lives not the man preaching the message.

The Bible teaches that when we sin, we need to confess and repent of our sin, then turn away from it and let go of it. We then need to ask God to forgive us of our sin through Jesus Christ.

"If we confess our sins, He is faithful and just to forgive us our sins and to cleanse us from all unrighteousness." (1 John. 1:9).

Even though God will forgive us of our sin, our influence or testimony may be destroyed forever. It is very hard to regain the trust of others after such a public failure. Even though Christ is willing to forgive us, there are still consequences of our sin. Both the Swaggart and Bakker ministries utterly were destroyed. Bakker eventually went to prison because of business improprieties in his ministry. His wife, Tammy Faye, divorced him and remarried while he was in prison and reportedly has battled health issues in recent years.

In the book of Second Samuel, we see that King David suffered greatly from the consequences of his sin against God. David took one of his soldiers' wives while the soldier was away from home at battle. His name was Uriah and his wife's name was Bathsheba. David took Uriah's wife as his own and had a sexual relationship with her. After she became pregnant, he ordered her husband home from war and then tried to get Uriah to sleep with his wife to cover David's own sin. But Uriah said that the Ark of God and the army of Israel were camped in the open fields and to honor God, his country and fellow soldiers, he would not go home and comfort himself with his wife.

When David's plan didn't work and he knew he would be exposed, he ordered his commanding general, Joab, to put Uriah in an unfavorable position in the war so that Uriah would be killed. After Uriah was killed, almighty God sent a prophet to David to confront him about his sins of adultery and murder. David confessed and repented of his sin. However, he still suffered severe consequences of his sin.

The son that was born to David and Bathsheba only lived for seven days, and then died. Another son Amnon raped his half sister Tamar, who was also David's daughter. Two years later yet another of David's sons, Absalom, got his brother Amnon drunk and commanded his servants to kill him for what he had done to Tamar. After Amnon's death, David allowed Absalom to return home and live in Jerusalem but he wouldn't allow Absalom to see him. Absalom became angry and set Joab's field on fire.

Absalom them rebelled against his father and many soldiers followed him in the revolt. David had to flee from his own son to save his life. David sent his loyal soldiers to fight Absalom and told Joab and the other commanders to deal gently with Absalom. However, Joab was still angry with Absalom for burning his barley field. So when he found Absalom caught in a terebinth tree he took three spears and thrust them through Absalom's heart.

God forgave David of his sin, but David suffered unbearable pain as a result of his sin. The son born to him and Bathsheba died. His son raped his daughter, and then two more of his sons were murdered. (2 Samuel Chapters 11-18, Psalm 51).

We were halfway around the world from home and I was reminded of a television preacher who had sinned in similar fashion to David. Fortunately, I would see a Christian man say no to sexual temptation with a beautiful woman before MacDonald and I left South Africa.

MacDonald was from Flint, Michigan, and had developed as a boxer while on the United States Marine Corps Boxing Team. After he was discharged from the Marines, he trained at Emanuel Steward's famed Kronk Gym in Detroit, Michigan. He turned professional in Phoenix, Arizona, and after a couple of matches he moved to Ft. Payne, Alabama, to train with former Marine boxing teammate, Lane Killien.

Lane introduced MacDonald to prominent Nashville, Tennessee, attorney Stan Allen. Allen was a very capable manager and promoter who worked very closely with Bob Arum of Top Rank, Inc. He also managed and promoted

Fight The Good Fight

1976 USA Olympic Team captain Clint "The Executioner" Jackson along with 1980 USA Olympic Trials silver medalist Jerome "Kid" Coffee. Allen began to manage and promote MacDonald. Jim and his lovely wife, Traci, moved to Nashville to further his career.

MacDonald wasn't the most skillful boxer, but he had a right hand that could knock out a mule. Whenever he was boxing, he would wait for his opponent to jab. Then, MacDonald would rock back on his right foot and counter his opponent's jab with that huge right hand. If he connected, the fight usually ended.

Allen put MacDonald on his boxing shows, and Jim started knocking fighters out left and right. He didn't have the amateur credentials of Jackson or Coffee so he wasn't rated, and the national media wasn't noticing him. Then Allen secured a fight for MacDonald against Willie Edwards, the No. 1-rated light-heavyweight boxer in the world. Luther Burgess trained Edwards at the Kronk Gym in Detroit. MacDonald had sparred with Edwards while training at Kronk and felt confident he could win the bout.

The two fighters met in Houston, Texas, on February 17, 1985. In the fourth round of the bout MacDonald caught Edwards with that big right hand and knocked him out. The win secured Diamond Jim a top-10 world ranking and a title fight against the great light-heavyweight champion Michael Spinks.

On June 6, 1985, MacDonald faced champion Spinks at the Las Vegas Rivera Hotel. Even though MacDonald was able to catch Spinks with his right hand and hurt him, Spinks never went down, but recovered and stopped MacDonald via a technical knockout in the eighth round.

Fight The Good Fight

Diamond Jim MacDonald, Michael Spinks and Kerry Pharr swap stories. Spinks was a former light-heavyweight and heavyweight world champion,

While MacDonald was in Nashville he and I became friends. I owned a health club there and managed junior welterweight Continental of America's champion Darryl "Fast Fists" Fuller. Even though Fuller was much smaller, he and Jim were frequent sparring partners. After his fight with Spinks and his contract with Allen ended, I briefly promoted MacDonald in 1988 and '89.

After we arrived at our hotel in Johannesburg and rested for a few hours, Jim Harvey came by the hotel to "collect us" as he phrased it. He took us to a very nice country club for a South African brie or barbeque. There were South African politicians, athletes and dignitaries there. Thinus Strydom informed us at the barbecue that the South African television

Fight The Good Fight

media wanted to get some footage of MacDonald boxing in a ring. They said that they would have someone for him to spar at the boxing gym in Jo-burg the next day.

When we arrived at the gym the next afternoon, the television reporters were there as well as the print media. They introduced us to the boxer who was scheduled to spar with MacDonald that day. I didn't feel comfortable that he would be sparring with someone we knew nothing about. It was about three weeks until the bout, but I didn't want to take any chance of MacDonald getting injured before the fight. I also felt as though the promoters were going to use their boxer to test my fighter. I told the promoters I would get dressed and spar with MacDonald so that the media could get some action tape on him, but that he wasn't going to spar with anyone else. We worked a couple of light rounds and the television crew got their footage for the evening news.

While in South Africa Thinus Strydom and Jim Harvey treated us like royalty. However, I knew that they were promoting Malinga and we were the supporting cast. Therefore I tried to look out for my guy the best that I could. The national media also treated us like we were VIP's. They wanted to know our opinions on everything and there were numerous press conferences as we helped the South Africans promote the upcoming show.

To generate interest in the upcoming bout with Malinga we were taken everywhere to hype the fight. At one of the press conferences I was standing next to our opponent, Malinga, as he was standing near the edge of a swimming pool. Malinga's promoter Jim Harvey whispered in my ear and encouraged me to push Malinga into the pool to generate more excitement for the upcoming bout. I had been around Malinga quite a bit while we were there, and he seemed to be a very humble, decent man. I thought, *"I'm from the richest country in the world. I'm not a wealthy person but the privileges and opportunities I've had in America are far greater than any Sugar Boy has ever had in South Africa."*

Thulane "Sugar Boy" Malinga was a Zulu tribesman born into abject poverty in a village in KwaZulu Natal, South Africa. Before he became a boxer, he never had been outside his own little community. He was becoming a national hero among the African tribesmen. His promoters were supporting him and later he would become a world champion, but he surely hadn't made a lot of money in his career when MacDonald fought him. I felt if I pushed him into the swimming pool it would be an incredible indignity to him. I wanted no part of insulting this decent man by pushing him into the pool.

While we were in Africa, we were taken to the hostels where the Xhosa, Zulu and Swazi tribesmen who worked in the gold mines lived. We also went to soccer fields and the boxers were introduced to large crowds. Before I left America I had filled a gym bag with Gideon New Testaments, courtesy of my good friend George Robinson. I'd brought them with me to give away.

When we arrived at a soccer field where several hundred Zulu tribesmen were assembled, Jim Harvey announced to the tribesmen on the loud speaker that I had Bibles to give them. The tribesmen ran out of the stands and mobbed me, trying to get to whatever this American man had in that bag.

I was amazed at how receptive the South Africans were to the Gospel of Jesus Christ, especially the black South Africans I met. They were a poor, yet very warm, gentle group of people. I told several of the teenage boys how Jesus died to save them and I asked if they would like to receive Christ as their savior. All of them eagerly responded "yes." We then prayed and they asked the Lord Jesus to forgive them or their sins and to be their Lord and savior. They walked away smiling, but about 15 minutes later, they returned with several other teenagers who also wanted to pray and ask Christ into their lives.

South African teenagers are shown just after accepting Jesus Christ as their Lord and savior.

Another time I was telling the maid in my hotel room about Jesus, and before I finished talking she fell to the floor on her knees to ask Christ into her heart. I had never seen such an eagerness to know about Christ.

The South African media made a star out of Diamond Jim in the short time we were there. The boxing match was to be held in Klerksdorf, South Africa, outdoors on a soccer field inside of Oppenheimer Stadium. We left Johannesburg for Klerksdorf two weeks before the fight.

When we arrived at our hotel in Klerksdorf, we saw a beautiful young woman who worked there. She had pretty blonde hair and gorgeous blue eyes. She became infatuated

Fight The Good Fight

with Diamond Jim. Jim was a young, muscular, handsome athlete who had been showcased on South African television almost from the moment we arrived.

Jim's wife, Traci, also was a very beautiful woman. She was at home in the United States with their two children. Jim loved them dearly. MacDonald was a Christian as well. He had struggled at times in his Christian life, especially when he was younger, but he truly wanted to live his life for Christ. This woman constantly followed Jim and me everywhere we went for the rest of our stay. She kept throwing herself at MacDonald. We were 6,000 miles from home and if MacDonald wanted to have a physical relationship with her, she was available. More than likely, no one in the U.S. would have ever known about it. Yet, again and again, I heard him tell her he was married and he wasn't going to fool around with her.

The night of the boxing match was March 7, 1988. When we arrived at Oppenheimer Stadium, we noticed the promotional efforts had paid off. As we entered the ring that night, the stands were filled to capacity with fans eager to see Sugar Boy Malinga and Diamond Jim MacDonald fight the 10-round main event.

MacDonald was in good shape, but struggled with the high altitude in South Africa during the fight. He appeared sluggish throughout the bout; however, he caught Malinga with a good right hand in about the seventh round and knocked Malinga down. Malinga got up off of the canvas to out-work and out-hustle MacDonald, earning a 10-round unanimous decision.

When the show ended and we arrived back at the hotel lobby the woman who was pursuing MacDonald, in a last ditch effort, threw herself at Jim. I heard "Mac" politely but sternly tell the woman, "I'm not going to go to bed with you. So forget it."

Fight The Good Fight

When we had arrived in South Africa three weeks earlier, our driver had asked me about Jimmy Swaggart. The very prominent American preacher who had spoken out against sexual immorality on television many times destroyed his testimony and hurt the cause of Christ when he fell into sin with a prostitute. His influence and reputation were forever tarnished around the world.

But on this trip, I saw a man say no to a very enticing woman because he wanted to be faithful to his Lord, his wife and his children. I admired him for his strength of character. MacDonald didn't win the bout against Malinga and he never became a world champion, but he didn't compromise and he didn't yield to temptation.

Several years later Malinga traveled to England and upset Nigel Benn to win the World Boxing Council super-middleweight world championship. Times had changed and so had South Africa. Nelson Mandela was now president of South Africa. Malinga arrived home from England to a hero's welcome and in celebration President Mandela pinned the world championship belt around Malinga's waist.

The Fighting Fireman

While I attended Tennessee Temple University in Chattanooga, Tennessee, in the mid-1970s, I befriended Don Bowman Sr. and his sons Don Jr. and Jeff. Don Sr. had been a rugged professional lightweight boxer in the early 1950s. He had been good enough to fight in two of boxing's great venues — Madison Square Garden and Sunnyside Gardens in New York. I was working in a health club that Don and his two sons were members of when I met them there.

Sometime later I was managing another health club in the city and I hired Don Jr. to be a personal trainer in the club. Don Jr. was the older son and wanted to box as an amateur. I trained him for a while during the time that I lived in Chattanooga. Don Jr. was a tall gifted athlete and would have become a very good boxer. However he loved body-building, and after a few amateur fights he gave up boxing and put his energy into bodybuilding.

Jeff the younger brother was a lean cross-country runner when I first met him while he was in high school. After I had moved to the Nashville area Jeff began to box. He boxed as an amateur for a couple of years then he turned professional and began boxing in the middleweight division. Over the next 15 years Jeff fought in tough man contests and professional boxing matches as well. He was a fearless road warrior who loved to fight. He never had a full-time trainer or a good boxing gym in which to train. However, he would literally take a fight on a moment's notice against anyone and travel to the city wherever the boxing match was and fight on sheer courage and determination. He fought on numerous shows that I promoted and always gave his all. He and Don Jr. were like younger brothers to me.

In his career Jeff fought 46 times professionally traveling all over the United States and even to Germany. Jeff fought from middleweight (160 lbs) to heavyweight (200 lbs and up). The married father of two was also a lieutenant in the Fire Department of his hometown.

Jeff died unexpectedly in March of 2006 in his sleep at age 42. Apparently he had a stomach aneurysm while he slept. Before retiring that night he responded to three incidents during his last shift at work as a fireman.

As a man and a fireman Jeff was a true all-American hero who loved to compete as a boxer. Jeff left behind a beautiful wife and two precious sons ages 11 and 16 that he was devoted to.

The boys lost their sweet Christian mother to brain cancer about six years before Jeff's passing. Don Sr. now is suffering from Alzheimer's disease. Don Jr. is a captain at the Chattanooga fire department and in his spare time he also manages a health club. He is still a bodybuilder and is fit enough to be featured in a men's health magazine.

'All He Has Left is Courage'

I began going to the boxing gym in Kenosha, Wisconsin, when I was about 15. I boxed in the local Golden Gloves and had been a sparring partner for numerous professional boxers in our area. I always wanted to be a professional boxer, but I got married at 20 and wasn't good enough to make a living as a boxer. So I got a job to support my wife and me. I was obsessed with boxing. Diane, my wife, came to hate boxing because of my abnormal love of the sport. It was what I lived and talked about from the time I got up each day until I went to bed each night. My work took me away from the boxing gym that I cherished. In every city that we lived in, I would find the local boxing gym and go work out whenever possible. For years, my dream of becoming a professional boxer was put on hold.

Then in 1981, when I was 32, I went to Memphis, Tennessee, to open and manage a new health club for a Nashville-based company.

I commuted from Nashville to Memphis during the week and returned home on weekends. While in Memphis, I went to the parks and recreation boxing gym at the fairgrounds and began training as a boxer again. Jimmy Heair, a professional boxer who had been rated in the top 10 in the world as a lightweight in the middle 1970s, had continued to box. Even though he had competed in more than 100 professional bouts and his skills had diminished significantly. He was 30 now and was boxing as a welterweight.

The first day I began training at the gym, Heair asked if I would spar with him. I hadn't sparred with a professional boxer in about seven years and was in terrible condition, so he wasn't able to get a lot of work out of me for several weeks. I would work for two or three rounds with him and have to get out of the ring because I ran out of gas.

Fight The Good Fight

I showed up every day at the gym, put my hand wraps, shorts, head gear and boxing gloves on and worked several rounds with Heair. He didn't want to use training gloves which were 16 ounces, but preferred to spar in fighting gloves, which were only 8 ounces. As I look back that was total insanity using fight gloves to spar with. It is so much easier to hurt someone with those small gloves on.

I would return the next day and we would do it all again day in, day out. It was about three months before I began to get in good enough shape to start holding my own. In the beginning, I weighed about 190 pounds and at the end of three months, I was down to 168 pounds. After three months, I'd gotten in good enough condition that I was able to run nine miles. Now that I was in shape, the sparring with Heair had become easy for me and I was seriously considering turning professional at age 32.

Heair had won 17 consecutive bouts while fighting in Memphis. Former World Boxing Association heavyweight champion Ernie Terrell was promoting boxing in Chicago, and he was promoting a welterweight by the name of Roosevelt Green. He contacted Heair by phone and offered him a fight against Green in Chicago. Heair accepted the bout and told me about it the next day at the gym.

"Kerry, I'm fighting Roosevelt Green in Chicago next month, would you go with me to Chicago and work my corner for the fight?" he asked me.

I had grown up 50 miles north of Chicago and I remembered seeing Green as an amateur. "I'll go with you and get a bunch of my friends to come down from Wisconsin to watch you fight," I told him.

We drove from Memphis to Chicago, then on to Kenosha, Wisconsin, where we stayed a couple of days with my cousin Phil before the bout. About a day before the fight we went to our hotel on Lakeshore Drive in Chicago.

Fight The Good Fight

Roosevelt Green came to the weigh-in, but was ill and couldn't fight Heair. Ernie Terrell scrambled and found a fighter from Indiana by the name of Charlie Peterson to face Heair. Here we were in Chicago on May 4, 1981, for a weigh-in for a professional boxing match. That night Heair won an easy 10-round decision against Peterson, a very ordinary fighter. Terrell booked Heair and his charge Roosevelt Green for his next show, which was scheduled for June 29.

Heair managed his own career and he would take fights on short notice and very close together without giving his body time to recuperate between bouts. After he left Chicago, he fought another fight just eight days later in Memphis, scoring a second-round KO against Tony Jordan. Three weeks later on June 6, he fought and won a 10-round unanimous decision against Don Morgan in Tupelo, Mississippi. Then on June 29, he faced Roosevelt Green in Chicago and lost a 10-round decision.

At about this time, I left Memphis and returned to Nashville, never again to consider a professional boxing career for myself. However, I was with Heair in Memphis six months later when he fought Bill "Fireball" Bradley in a 10-round main event at the Cook Convention Center.

That night we shared a dressing room with Irish Billy Collins Jr. of Nashville. It was his second professional fight, and he was a really good-looking prospect. His dad, Billy Sr., had been a welterweight contender in the late 1950s and early 1960s, and had fought future welterweight world champion and hall of famer Curtis Cokes for the Southern welterweight championship, losing on a 10-round decision. Earlier in his career Billy Sr. also had given "Irish" Bobby Cassidy of New York his first professional loss in his career. Cassidy later ended up being a top light-heavyweight contender.

Cassidy had been at my house in Tennessee when he was in town with former light heavyweight champion Donnie Lalonde. "I was just a kid when I fought Billy Collins and

206

Fight The Good Fight

he was already a tough veteran. When I walked past his dressing room the night of the fight and looked in, he was sound asleep. That really scared me," Cassidy said to me.

Now Collins' son was fighting professionally and he looked like a real comer as he scored a second-round KO against Gary Baker on January 19,1982.

Heair was beaten in a decision that night and he was beginning to look shopworn.

That's why boxing commissions need to protect boxers. Many of the fighters do not know when to quit. Ali and former heavyweight champion Evander Holyfield are two of the all-time greatest heavyweight fighters, yet they kept boxing long after their skills had seriously eroded. Fortunately, New York State Boxing Commissioner Ron Scott Stevens had the courage to suspend Holyfield's license late in his career, after watching him in a sub-par performance in a fight against Larry Donald in Madison Square Garden. Unfortunately, other states licensed him and allowed him to continue boxing. He still fights to this day, chasing his dream of regaining his world title.

It's obvious to everyone but the fighter. It's very evident when a boxer becomes a shell of his younger self. "He is a shot fighter" is a term often used to describe a boxer whose skills are gone. For their own protection, a boxer should retire long before their body reaches this condition. But they can't see it happening. The limelight, the fame and the glory is like a drug, and it is extremely hard to for a boxer to walk away from it. I was in the dressing room with Jimmy Heair, the night he lost the first fight of his career that he wasn't competitive in. During the fight, I heard someone at ringside say, "All he has left is courage." They could see his skill was gone and unfortunately I was there to witness it, also.

After the fight, Heair began sobbing in the dressing room. "I hate to quit boxing. It's the only thing that made my life special. It's the only thing that separated me from the guy digging a ditch," he said.

I never worked his corner again because I couldn't stand to see this happening to him. Many friends in and out of boxing encouraged him to hang up his gloves and call it a career.

Against the advice of all of these people, Heair continued to box for several more years and probably would have never retired if he still could have gotten a license. That's the reason that boxing commissions were established, to regulate the sport and most importantly to protect the boxers. Fighters without competitive skills or who have diminished skills shouldn't be allowed to fight.

'Baby' Ortiz

Benito "Benny" Ortiz, who was a stablemate of three-time world champion Emile Griffith and was managed by Boxing Hall of Fame manager/trainer Gil Clancy, rose to prominence as a world-class featherweight in the 1960s. In fact, Benny's skill and drawing power earned four appearances in the ring at the famous Madison Square Garden venue in New York City. Benny, who was a smooth-as-silk, fluid, mobile boxer, developed a boxing style that he referred to as Spanish dancing. During his boxing career Benito was nicknamed "Baby" Ortiz.

After his career as a fighter, Benny became a professional boxing trainer in his native Puerto Rico. Eventually, Benny became the head trainer and manager of the renowned Times Square Gym in New York owned by Jimmy Glenn, who was Benny's former trainer. As a trainer, Benny's forte was teaching boxers how to glide gracefully around the ring. He taught them his Spanish dancing style of movement. During training sessions, Benny used salsa dance steps to show his boxers how to maneuver right and left, in and out, by pivoting off of both feet.

Keith McKnight, a quick, mobile heavyweight with more than 40 wins, learned his moves from Benny. When Bobby Goodman worked as the matchmaker at the Garden, he would send boxers scheduled to fight at the famed arena to see Benny to train while in New York.

Benny gained quite a reputation as a wild man in his boxing days. He will tell you that he loved to party, drink, gamble and dance all night in the Puerto Rican clubs in Spanish Harlem. Others who knew Benny at the time have said that Benny made no qualms about settling his differences with a gun or a knife, if necessary.

Early one morning in 1992, Benny staggered home following a marathon session of drinking and partying. He

Fight The Good Fight

found himself burdened with a heavy guilt beyond any he had ever experienced before about the way he was living. Benny began to realize he was in danger of losing his lovely wife, Sonja, and his two sons, Benito Jr. and Owen. During his reflection, something provoked Benny to turn on the radio, where he heard a preacher telling people to give their lives to Jesus Christ. The preacher invited his radio audience to pray and ask Christ to save them from their sin. Benito called the radio preacher at 4 a.m. to say, "My name is Benito Ortiz, and I need to get saved." As the preacher prayed with him, Benito gave his life to Christ.

From that day forward, Benito never looked back. He relinquished his job at New York's Times Square Gym, along with the booze, gambling and the street fighting. He began to devote his life to telling others about how Christ changed his life. Today, Benito lives his life as a happy disciple of Christ. If you were to meet Benito today, you would see a man with a joyful glow in his face, a happy bounce in his step and a love for others in his soul. He still lives in New York's Spanish Harlem at 114th and Lexington with his beautiful wife. Ironically, Benito and his family live in an apartment next door to the mother of former world champion Hector "Macho" Camacho. Benito's sons are happily married and living in Orlando, Florida. Benito remains very active in his church, preaching and singing whenever he is asked.

The Mayor of Lower Broadway

The tall, muscular, tobacco-chewing man, wearing complete western gear topped off with a cowboy hat walked into my boxing gym during the summer of 1991. He was in his 50s then; his name was Robert Moore. He had brought along one of the heavyweight boxers he managed to spar. His fighter sparred several rounds with Keith McKnight. After being roughed up by McKnight, we never saw the boxer again. Robert, we later learned, was something of a legend on Nashville's Lower Broadway. He had rolled into town some 15 years earlier from West Tennessee, where he had been a deputy sheriff for Buford Pusser, the McNairy County, Tennessee, sheriff made famous by the movie *Walking Tall*.

Robert originally was hired to regulate the thugs in the rough part of downtown Nashville. He began his career as a bouncer at the Merchants' Bar on Lower Broadway. Through the years, he was cited 62 different times for assault while breaking up fights. Some West Tennesseans claimed he could have whipped the legendary Pusser, a mammoth 6-foot-6 man. The story is told by those who worked for him in Nashville that during an all-out brawl by a motorcycle gang in his bar, Robert plunged into the crowd and started throwing the drunken revelers out by himself. One of his employees offered to call the police to which Robert replied, "This is my bar. I don't need the police. I'll take care of it myself."

He subsequently broke up the fight and restored order by himself.

Eventually he bought and sold many businesses on Broadway. He owned the famous Tootsie's Orchid Lounge across the alley from the Ryman Auditorium, historic home of the Grand Ole Opry, where the country music stars hung their hats between shows. He also owned Robert's Western

World, a bar on Broadway that provided live country music and sold cowboy boots in the same location.

Robert was a gentle, good-hearted man who would do almost anything to help others. Every Thanksgiving and Christmas, he cooked a feast at his business for the homeless. However, if you provoked him, he could become angry and violent very quickly. Although his lifestyle was different than mine, Robert and I became close friends through the years. During this time, he became a prominent boxing manager/promoter in Nashville.

Many times I told Robert about Jesus Christ, my Lord and Savior, and that I was praying for him to give his life to Christ. For the most part he ignored me; other times he would argue with me, but I could tell he heard what I was saying. He developed and promoted some very good local boxers, including World Boxing Federation cruiserweight champions Joey Guy and Mike "The Honkytonk Hitman" Rodgers, Karl Willis, world title challenger Frankie Swindell and Bobby Elkins.

After spending 30 years on lower Broad, Robert was known and affectionately called "The Mayor of Lower Broadway." Today, the former war zone has been revitalized and is a huge tourist attraction. Robert sold his last bar on Broadway in 1998, and closed his last business on Broadway, a check cashing company called Mr. Cash, in 2001.

Several months later, he collapsed while at work at a truck stop he owned and was taken to the hospital where he was diagnosed with brain cancer. The prognosis wasn't good and Robert's chances of surviving were very slim. I visited him in the hospitable and I asked him if he would like to ask Jesus Christ to be his Lord and Savior. He assured me he had prayed and given his life to Christ.

The surgeon operated on him, but told his family members before the surgery that there was little hope for his survival. We all stood by, nervously dreading word that Robert had

Fight The Good Fight

died. Unbelievably and miraculously, he survived and is alive as I write these words. The doctors told him several months ago that the cancer had returned, and again the prognosis wasn't good. Now 70, the rough-and-tough Robert Moore got a job as a security officer several years ago and continues to press on, working 55-65 hours a week.

In January 2007, Robert was selected as security officer of the year out of 186 security guards for City Wide security. Recently at the church he attends, he gave a report of his grim prognosis. Those in attendance said they would pray for Robert, who asked them not to pray for him to be healed, but rather to pray for him to go to heaven when he dies.

Boxing's Treacherous Road

For those who never have managed or trained a professional boxer, the goal of the manager is to develop a fighter to the best of his ability. And for those young men wishing to fight professionally, there are some things you need to know before you begin your career in the professional ranks. Most boxers have amateur experience before attempting to fight professionally. The best professional boxers are usually those who started at an early age in the amateurs. Many of these athletes start in the sport as early as eight to 10 years of age. By the time these youngsters are 18–20, they are veteran boxers with 10 years of experience. Muhammad Ali started boxing at age 12 and won six Kentucky Golden Gloves Championships, at least three national championships and an Olympic gold medal. Sugar Ray Leonard began as a youngster, as did Thomas "Hit Man" Hearns and Oscar De La Hoya. Each of them had a minimum of 150 amateur bouts and won numerous local, regional and national championships before fighting professionally. Leonard and De La Hoya captured Olympic gold at the Montreal and Los Angeles Olympics, respectively. If you are a boxer with limited experience there's virtually no way you can compete against fighters with this amount of experience.

Kerry Pharr, left, Ray Leonard and Keith McKnight visit after a McKnight bout.

These fighters with amateur experience have honed their skills and become battle hardened in a multitude of championships in the course of their teenage years. The best thing you can do is to remain an amateur until you have gained enough experience to compete at a high level. If you want to compete on a world-class level as a professional boxer, you need to gain experience as an amateur. Preferably, you need to win some major amateur titles. If you aren't good enough to win a local Golden Gloves tournament, then odds are you have no business boxing as a professional. As a rule, the great professional boxing champions won numerous national and Olympic championships. A loss as an amateur does not decrease your value as a boxer, whereas a loss in the professional ranks does. An undefeated professional boxer always has more value than a boxer with losses on his record. However, never make the mistake of assuming a fighter with a bad record is a bad fighter, or a fighter with a good record is a good fighter. Some fighters are 10-0, but the record is deceiving because they have not faced a decent opponent. On the other hand, a fighter with a record of 11-11 may be one tough customer.

A talented boxer who becomes a professional is called a prospect. If he puts together a string of wins and is undefeated after 15 or 16 bouts, he is considered a good prospect. If that fighter loses several bouts, he is then considered an opponent and no longer a prospect. An opponent is the type of fighter that other managers use to develop their prospects.

There is a process of developing a boxer from an amateur to a prospect into a good prospect, into a contender and ultimately a world champion. The prospect is ordinarily untested because his wins have come against boxers who are considered opponents. To graduate from the ranks of a prospect into a contender, one has to beat a fighter who is also considered a contender or win a regional title like the Continental of Americas Championship, United States Boxing Association or North American Boxing Federation championship against a worthy opponent. These are regional titles that are a step or two below a world title.

A contender is viewed as one having the ability to contend or be competitive against the world champion. There are steps you have to climb in the sport of professional boxing. Obviously, the ultimate dream as a boxing manager or trainer is to help your boxer win a World Championship, and to earn millions of dollars to help him and you become financially secure.

Fight The Good Fight

In boxing, very few fighters make the type of money you read about the superstars making in the newspaper. I would venture to say that maybe only two percent of professional boxers make significant money from boxing. You can count on your hands the number of million dollar fighters in the sport of boxing.

As a boxing manager, trainer and promoter for 20-plus years, I never made enough money to quit my day job. I never managed anyone who became famous or earned enough money to quit his job long term. Most of my boxers' biggest paydays were in the $20,000 to $25,000 range. As a manager I generally received one-third of the purse or about $8,300 on a $25,000 fight. Out of that I paid the trainer's expenses of 10 percent and the cut-man's expenses of 2 percent plus a number of other expenses along the way (phone, equipment, sparring partners, travel, meals, etc.). Believe me, when I retired from boxing, I'd spent more money on the boxers through the years than I had made. Most trainers and managers work in the game for the love of the kids, the love of the sport and a little notoriety. Occasionally, you are quoted in the newspaper or you are seen on television with your boxer and although it's a little fix, it is still like a drug that you enjoy and can't get enough of. That's why the great boxers have such a hard time walking away while they are on top. Almost none of them retire undefeated because the roar of the crowd, the media coverage, the attention and the adulation of the fans inflate their egos to the point that they are consumed by megalomania. They just can't stand to move away from the spotlight, the allure of glory.

In the beginning, most debuting professional boxers who haven't won an Olympic gold medal are fighting for as little as a $100 per round, or $400 for a four-round fight. Out of that meager purse, license fees are deducted; the manager and trainer also get a percentage. Many times a boxer ends up with half or less for himself. Many managers are noto-rious for stealing from their boxers.

I knew a Cuban manager who lived in Miami. He would bring boxers in from Latin countries and put them in tough fights so he could make more money for himself. Before I knew this about him, I helped him work in the corner for one of his fighters in Nashville, Tennessee, in the early 1980s. His fighter was facing bantamweight contender Jerome "Kid" Coffee in the 10-round main event of a show that my good friend Stan Allen promoted. Allen promoted Coffee, 1976 U.S. Olympic team captain Clint Jackson, Diamond Jim MacDonald as well as many others.

Coffee was a former national amateur champion and a silver medalist in the USA Olympic Trials. He was a master boxer. The Latin fighter was in a very tough fight. My recol-lection is that the manager was paid $2,500 for the boxer after the fight. He gave the poor unsuspecting South American fighter $500 and kept $2,000 for himself. I believe he offered me $20 for helping him that night. I told him, "No thanks."

I couldn't believe how exploitive this manager was. This was not only immoral, but also criminal. He justified taking that amount of money from the boxer because he had paid the fighters expenses to America and was supporting him while he was here. Since that time federal laws, like the Muhammad Ali Act, have been enacted to circumvent this from happening to boxers. However, things similar to this on a much larger scale happen in professional boxing today.

If you are a young man wanting to box professionally, make sure that whoever you choose as your manager isn't the type of person who will use and abuse you. Additionally a boxing manager needs to know something about the sport. He needs to understand how to develop and move a boxer's career forward. I can't say that I was a great manager, because I never developed anyone who made it into big-time boxing or became wealthy. But the guys who stayed with me and

Fight The Good Fight

trusted me with their careers ended up with great records, made some money, won respectable titles and had a lot of fun and traveled all around the world. They were developed to the best of their abilities.

Even though there are unscrupulous boxing managers, on the flip side of the coin, there are also good managers who will spend thousands of dollars, even hundreds of thousands of dollars, for several years without taking a percentage of the boxer's purse. They will set up some type of draw where they subsidize the boxer until the purses are large enough for the manager to recoup some of his investment and still allow the athlete decent paydays. These are generally the wealthy businessmen who manage what I'll refer to as first-tier boxers. These boxers are those who have won Olympic medals or major national, amateur titles.

Most second and third-tier boxers cannot earn a living in the early days of their careers by boxing alone. Nearly all of them have full-time jobs and use the boxing matches to supplement their income. Most trainers and managers are also working a full-time job and are managing and training boxers on a part-time basis. These managers and trainers cannot afford to supplement their fighters. Nor can they afford to pay thousands of dollars a week for sparring partners for their fighters like the million dollar world champions do. Some top-notch champions pay as much as $1,500 a week to each sparring partner. These part-time boxers, managers and trainers are strictly working class people. Such was my lot as a trainer and manager. For the entire time I was a boxing trainer, I worked a full-time job during the day to make a living. In the evening, I would meet the boxers at the gym, which would be open for about three hours. We would travel to or host boxing shows on the weekend. For professional bouts I would use vacation time to travel with my boxers.

I started an amateur boxing program in the early 1980s as a way to minister to the kids in my area. As an outgrowth of that program we developed some talented amateur and professional boxers.

Some managers recognize the limitations of their boxers and use them as opponents. An opponent is someone who will take a bout on a day's notice. Many opponents and their managers don't care if they win or lose. They are strictly fighting for the payday. I must say that there have been some great opponents who made a great deal of money as such. They are rare. There was a tremendous boxing trainer, who is now dead, in our area who had the philosophy that after six or seven fights a fighter should be fighting against world-class boxers. He had great ability as a trainer and could teach a boxer how to fight very quickly and very skillfully. Through the years I watched him take fighters with tremendous talent and put them in above their heads long before they were ready. He would load them into his white Cadillac and they would travel all across the country fighting fighters who would become great world champions, whenever he got the call. All of his boxers ended up being washed-up opponents almost overnight. With his ability as a trainer there's no way of knowing what great champion he might have developed had he not been so greedy and cared at all about those whom he worked with.

I was a different type of manager. I thought that I could take my athletes and develop them into world-class boxers. Therefore, I was more selective in whom I would allow them to fight. This type of development takes time and a manager like this isn't going to put a boxer in above his head before he believes he is ready. There is a nurturing process that has to take place. An analogy that I like to use is that of planting an acorn. When it first sprouts it isn't very strong or durable. But given time to be toughened by many storms one day it becomes a powerful giant oak tree. I wanted to nurture and develop our athletes so we could take the fighter as far as his ability would allow him to go. We carefully maneuvered our

Fight The Good Fight

boxers with the hope of getting a world title fight for them. This process is delicate and can be carried to the extreme. Some fighters become protected and never face decent opposition. They build up pretty records but have little substance behind them. Then, when they face a good fighter, they are not prepared.

Most of the athletes that we started with were local or regional champions. None of them had competed in the Olympics or won an Olympic medal. It is very rare that a boxer rises from this level to win a world championship or becomes wealthy or famous. Something that I didn't realize then – which I do now – is that a second- or third-tier boxer has as good a chance at winning the lottery as he does at becoming a multi-million dollar fighter. There is only one exception to the rule that I remember and that was Canadian Donnie LaLonde. Aside from him, I don't remember a single boxer who didn't win a national title that became both a world champion and a multi-million dollar fighter. There were several who won championships but didn't earn a lot of money. It is very rare that a boxer without an amateur pedigree goes on to win it all. In spite of the overwhelming odds against us, the boxers and I labored for many years in a sweaty, boxing gym, chasing that elusive dream. I loved working with the kids and, as I've already mentioned, I enjoyed the little bit of notoriety it brought to our guys and myself.

We didn't have the money to sign Olympic-class talent. So we developed the athletes we had with years of hard work in our own gym. Our most decorated amateur was Adam Richards, who won four Junior Olympic National titles. Adam also competed in the 2000 Olympic Trials Box-offs, but lost by a decision in the tournament's second round.

Mr. Boxing Manager, if your goal is to build a professional boxer it is a very slow, hard, laborious process. To develop a professional boxer you have to book your athlete on other promoters' boxing cards or become a promoter yourself. If you choose to allow your boxer to fight on other promoter's shows the deck is stacked against you. Your athlete has to become a road warrior. Your boxer has to fight on the other promoter's show usually against his house fighter, in their hometown. The local boxer has a fan base who's there cheering their fighter on and many local judges are partial and inclined to give the local kid the decision should the bout go the distance. (There are a few good local judges, though.)

In some ways developing a professional boxer is similar to playing chess. If you make the wrong move, you get jumped and you are out of the game, finished and washed up. I've often felt that maneuvering a boxer is like swimming in shark-infested waters. There are sharks all along the way trying to devour you and your prospect. Many promoters invite you to their shows and try to sign away your fighters. Boxing is replete with envious and jealous people waiting to jump you and steal an athlete that you've spent 10 years of your life nurturing and developing. Many trainers work for years without any pay, day in and day out, driving a carload of teenagers to amateur shows every weekend. By the time a fighter is ready to fight professionally the amateur coach has spent 3,000 - 4,000 hours in the gym with him, traveled 15,000 to 20,000 miles on the road, paid his and the boxers traveling expenses and invested thousand of dollars of his own money in the fighter.

Around every corner there are unscrupulous, amoral managers and promoters enticing boxers with promises to leave you. I've had boxers tell me that another promoter, manager or trainer would say, "What are you doing with that bum? Just think how far you could go without him." Or, "I'll promote you, but you have to leave your manager behind."

Imagine that you are a boxing manager and your goal is to keep your athlete from defeat. Just like a football or

Fight The Good Fight

basketball coach you're trying to get to the championship. If your fighter gets beat before he gets on national television or in a championship fight, he doesn't earn much money. An undefeated fighter can command much more money than a fighter who has losses on his record. As a manager you want to put your boxer in contests that will develop his skill and improve his world ranking. Along the way you spend thousands of dollars and years of your life trying to keep your fighter undefeated so you can get him in a big money fight. You try desperately to get him rated as one of the top 10 fighters in the world. Once you get him rated in the top 10, you are just a win or two from the ultimate prize, a shot at the world championship and maybe a million-dollar fight.

In your path are not only tough fighters, but also promoters and boxing matchmakers who get a tremendous amount of satisfaction in personally getting your fighter beat.

Teddy Brenner, the famous Madison Square Garden matchmaker said, "he could get any fighter beat."

I've heard it said that he enjoyed getting undefeated fighters beat. In fact he loved it. I've heard others say. Teddy was so good at it that he came close to getting a young Cassius Clay beat in Madison Square Garden when he pitted him against Doug Jones. Young Cassius barely escaped with a disputed split decision that night but went on to become Muhammad Ali, the self-proclaimed greatest heavyweight of all time. Even the greatest of all boxers need time to develop and hone their boxing skills after they leave amateur boxing and enter the pro-ranks.

In my opinion, New Yorker, Dave Wolf was one of the greatest boxing managers in the history of the sport. Wolf, a former sportswriter worked for Heavyweight Champion Joe Frazier before he became a boxing manager. He handled the boxing careers of lightweight world Champion Ray "Boom Boom" Mancini, light heavyweight World Champion Donnie LaLonde, Middleweight Champion Lonnie Bradley

Fight The Good Fight

and even football player-turned-boxer Ed "Too Tall" Jones. Wolf and I worked together for a while and he was a great mentor to me. I tried to emulate his managing style and did so with a modicum of success, but I wasn't Dave Wolf. Very few managers have equaled his success in the sport.

Wolf told me the following story. Yank Durham, the manager of Joe Frazier, was offered a $50,000 fight for Joe against heavyweight contender Jerry Quarry early in his career. This offer was a tremendous amount of money in the 1960s; however Yank thought that Quarry was too experienced for Joe at that time. He explained to Frazier that he thought Quarry would still be around a couple of years later and they would make a lot more money by fighting Quarry then. Durham turned the fight down, and sure enough, Frazier and Quarry fought for the Heavyweight Championship of the world a couple of years later. Frazier won the fight by stopping Quarry and earned 10 times as much as that first offer. Dave Wolf was as proficient as a manager that he was able to develop Donnie LaLonde, an ordinary fighter, with a canon for a right hand, into a world champion and a $7,000,000 payday against "Sugar" Ray Leonard. Wolf was a master at negotiation. Getting his fighter the perfect bout at the right time and for the maximum amount of money was his forte.

Keith McKnight, left, poses for a photo with the great former world champion Sugar Ray Leonard.

A good manager protects his charge but conversely the boxing matchmaker's job is to make a fight extremely competitive so that the fans will see a pier six brawl between the two combatants. Too many fight cards are filled with mismatches. Fans deserve to see competitive bouts. The fans will love the exciting bout the matchmaker has made and will want to buy tickets to see another boxing show. When the matchmaker is trying to make a match he will always undersell your opponent and even outright lie to you about the opponent your boxer is facing in order to get you to accept the fight. If he were to tell you he thinks your fighter is going to be in a war and that he'll probably lose the bout, there's no chance a good manager would agree to the fight unless the money for the bout is extremely large or he doesn't care about his fighter.

A good manager does not want to get his fighter beat, he attempts to do four things with his boxer (1) don't get him hurt (2) keep him unbeaten. (3) Win a world championship or develop him into a million dollar fighter. (4) Don't overprotect him and gradually move him up against better competition.

A matchmaker trying to sell me on a match for my fighter would say, "Oh, he's an ordinary fighter who walks straight in, he's not a puncher, it's a good fight for your guy."

Then after we'd agreed to the bout and my fighter was in the ring with the matchmaker's boxer, he would be an extraordinary fighter, who never walked in straight, could move like Muhammad Ali and punch like Mike Tyson.

As a manager, you end up in an adversarial role with your promoter and your matchmaker. Once you get a fighter's record built to the point that he is capable of fighting a 10-round main event, you generally can get a contract with a major promoter to put your boxer in televised fights. The promoter's job is to develop your fighter. Even though they are supposedly promoting your boxer, they might sign 20 other boxers in your fighter's weight division at the same time.

So the word "promoter" is actually an oxymoron. Most promoters pit their own boxers against each other. They actually put them in a situation similar to an elimination tournament where the promoter eliminates the very fighters he is supposed to be developing. The promoter doesn't care because he keeps the winner under his promotional wing and in the event the boxer fights for a major title or payday the promoter gets a sizable portion of his purse. The promoter

Fight The Good Fight

has a clause in each boxer's contract that allows him to rescind all of his obligations to the fighter, or to drop him from his promotional agreement if he loses a bout. Often the promoter drops the losing boxer completely.

Aside from all of this, the television money is very attractive to your fighter and you. Sometimes your fighter asks you to make an extremely tough match for him and reluctantly you accept a bout for him that you know isn't the best fight for him at that particular time because the money you've been offered is so good. However if you are fortunate enough to manage someone with great talent and skill like a Leonard, Hearns, De La Hoya or Ali, it rarely matters against whom he's matched. The cream will rise to the top regardless of who his manager, trainer or promoter is. The great fighter wins tough fights and championships, earns millions of dollars and makes those around him look great. He makes everyone believe they are the best at what they do and are the smartest people in the world.

It was tough being a Christian who tried to live by Christlike principles while involved in the seedy sport of boxing. It was really difficult to use principles of honesty and integrity while nearly everyone else was using a different set of rules. I spent more than half of my life involved in the sport and when I left I took nothing with me but memories. In my tenure in the sport I was an amateur boxer and coach, a professional trainer, a boxing manager and a boxing promoter. I served on the State of Tennessee's boxing advisory board for six years. I tried to utilize Christian principles of honesty and integrity in my business dealings. I did my best to treat everyone with respect and I proclaimed the Gospel of Jesus Christ whenever and wherever I could.

I would have loved to seen what I could have done as a manager or trainer of an Olympic-champion fighter.

I was deeply saddened by some of the guys that I had worked with for years. I had done much for these young

227

men. However, some of them walked away from me as a manager without even talking to me or showing any appreciation for what I had done for them, or caring about my feelings. In retrospect I can see God even working in those circumstances for it allowed me the freedom to break away from the sport and pursue other things God had in store for me. *And we know that all things work together for good to those who love God, to those who are the called according to his purpose.* Romans 8:28

I was involved in a sport that had me unequally yoked as a Christian and I probably should have walked away much sooner than I did (2 Corinthians 6:14). I won't know until I meet Christ if I was able to minister to any of the young men I worked with for all those years or if it was a waste of time.

I spent years of my life teaching young men how to defend themselves through the sport of boxing. That knowledge or training only benefits a person temporarily.

My heart's desire for the rest of my life is to do something that will benefit people eternally, and that is to point them to Jesus Christ. He, "Jesus," promises eternal life in a wonderful place called heaven to those who acknowledge and accept him as Lord and Savior. Those who have received him into their lives have a reservation written down in the logbooks of heaven. I've got my reservation. I invite you to receive yours, too.

Chapter 8: Depression and Addictions

'There's No Padding in These … Gloves!'

I first met boxer Irish Billy Ray Collins in Memphis, Tennessee, on January 19, 1982. One of the professional boxers I was working with was fighting in the 10-round main event that night, and we shared a dressing room with the young Collins. His father, Billy Sr., was a world class welterweight professional boxer in the 1960s. The younger Collins had a good amateur career and now was competing in his second professional bout, a fight he won via a second-round knockout against Gary Baker. Collins was a good-looking boxing prospect. His dad was his manager and trainer.

Since Collins lived in the Nashville area where I lived, I followed his career with great interest. I introduced the Collins' to Randy Weiler, a friend of mine from church and a sports writer with *The Nashville Banner*. Randy wrote the first newspaper article and others on the young prospect. Collins was undefeated and moving up the professional boxing ranks very rapidly. Because of his dad's notoriety he landed a promotional agreement with Bob Arum's Top Rank Inc, arguably the best promotional boxing company in the world. All of Collins' fights now would be televised on

ESPN. Top Rank was grooming him for stardom and a world championship fight.

Collins had a professional record of 14 wins with no losses when Top Rank decided to showcase him in a nationally televised match from Madison Square Garden. He would be fighting on the undercard of the legendary champion Roberto Duran, who was fighting Davey Moore for the World Boxing Association light middleweight world championship.

Collins entered the ring before a capacity crowd of more than 20,000 fans on June 16, 1983, a heavy favorite against the lightly regarded journeyman Luis Resto. Astonishingly, early in the fight, Resto began to batter Collins, whose eyes horribly were swollen. Even though Collins was considered the much better fighter, Resto continued to punish Collins the entire 10 rounds.

Throughout the fight, something looked strangely out of sync with Collins. His injuries were far greater than a boxer usually absorbed in a match with gloves on. Billy Sr. felt that something terribly was wrong and walked to Resto's corner at the end of the bout to shake hands with him. He instantly felt there was no padding in Resto's gloves, and he began screaming and cursing at the officials and press members sitting at ringside.

"There's no padding in these   - gloves!"

The gloves were taken off Resto and impounded by the New York State Athletic Commission. It later was determined the padding had been removed from the gloves by Panama Lewis, Resto's trainer.

Today, boxing gloves are padded with high density foam; boxing gloves then were padded with horsehair. Lewis had taken a pair of tweezers and meticulously removed the horsehair padding from each glove in the dressing room before the bout. Unfortunately, no one from the Collins camp or the

Fight The Good Fight

New York State Athletic Commission inspected the gloves before the fight.

Resto received a unanimous 10-round decision against Collins. Resto and Lewis were arrested and later tried and convicted of conspiracy to fix a fight and other crimes. Lewis spent a year in prison and was banned from the sport of boxing for life in America by the New York State Athletic Commission. Resto spent 2½ years in prison and also was banned from the sport. The commission subsequently ruled the bout a no-contest and restored Collins' record to 14-0.

Collins received permanent eye damage and vision impairment in the fight and was told he never would be able to box again. According to friends and family members, he went into a state of depression. Nine months later on March 7, 1984, he was at a Nashville bar with a friend, John Duke, and Billy Sr. Reportedly, Collins had too much to drink, and as he was about to leave the bar, his father took his car keys and handed them to Duke and asked him to drive his son home.

When Collins and Duke walked outside the bar, Billy asked John to give his keys back to him. Just a few minutes later, at approximately 1 a.m., Collins was driving his Oldsmobile west on Old Franklin Road in Nashville when his car veered down an embankment into a creek and landed upside down. Collins was killed while Duke walked away with minor injuries.

Only 23, Billy Collins had a very promising future as an undefeated professional boxer only to have it stolen from him.

Dealing with Depression

Depression, drinking and speeding were all factors that reportedly contributed to Irish Billy Collins' early death. Depression is a terrible thing to face, but it's not something worth losing your life about. Depression strikes about 17 million American adults each year – more than cancer, AIDS or coronary heart disease – according to the National Institute of Mental Health. An estimated 15 percent of chronic depression cases end in suicide. Women are twice as likely as men to be affected.

Drinking alcohol when you are depressed is like playing Russian roulette. The feelings of depression sometimes make you lose your will to live and alcohol clouds your judgment causing a person to take risks with their life.

Obviously, I'm not a doctor or a psychologist. In fact, I think I earned a C- in my only college psychology class. So I'm not qualified to treat anyone, let alone someone who needs professional help. I'm just offering what little I've learned from my own life experiences and from studying the word of God, hoping that my two cents worth might be an inspiration to someone who's hurting. And I know that if you apply God's word to your life it will help you to heal.

If you are depressed, the good news is that you can do something about it. Don't mix alcohol or drugs with depression. Get up and do something to get you out of the doldrums. Exercise is good medicine for the body and the mind. There is an abundance of help available.

After I lost my first wife Diane to breast cancer, I went into a state of depression. I cried every day for six weeks. I would think of my wife and begin to cry. The crying was like a sprinkler system that would automatically go off. I couldn't control it, and that was good because it allowed me to grieve and begin healing emotionally at the same time.

Fight The Good Fight

Even men who are considered tough – those who have played football, or climbed into a boxing ring and fought their hearts out – get depressed and break down and cry. They are human beings, not heartless robots made of steel. Early on, boys are taught to be a man and not to cry. Athletes in pain are constantly told to be tough and "suck it up." Boxers in particular are trained to never show pain or fear because their opponent can sense their weaknesses and knock them out while they temporarily are unable to defend themselves.

When you are hurting emotionally, crying helps to release all of those feelings and it helps to heal the pain and depression. After a period of time though, we all need to quit feeling sorry for ourselves and get up off of the couch or bed and move on.

For a while, I thought I was going insane while I was depressed. A noted author said, "The statistics on sanity are that one out of every four American's is suffering from some form of mental illness. Think of your three best friends. If they are OK, then it's you."

Putting the aforementioned humor aside, even if you think it is you who are suffering from some form of mental illness, it's OK. You can get help and you can get well. Yes you can! Sure you can! God can provide healing for you!

In reality, depression is a form of mental illness. I didn't want to stay depressed so I did something to help alleviate the depression. I read the Bible, I prayed, I went to church and got involved with other people. I joined a health club and began working out.

Years ago a good friend said to me, "If God made anything better than a woman, he kept it for himself. I believe if I ever lost my wife I'd go get me another one."

In reality, he was expressing how wonderful life was with his precious wife. I had also been blessed with a great wife. Even though I missed my wife immensely, I knew Diane was all right because she was in heaven, and I didn't want to be alone for the rest of my life. I had experienced life with a wonderful mate and I longed for that type of loving relationship again.

So in my 50s I started dating and several months later met a wonderful Christian woman named Lanita. She and I dated for about six months and then we married. God filled a void in my life by giving me another lovely wife.

Life is a cycle of ups and downs, very similar to the waves of the ocean. If you are at the bottom of a wave and are depressed and hurting, do something positive to help ease and ultimately heal the pain. Don't worry about what others will say or think about you, take care of yourself. Be aggressive and do something for yourself. Don't just sit around and wait for help because it never will come that way. Be proactive and do something that will help you to heal emotionally and physically as well.

Many people try to be tough and to handle these circumstances on their own when they need help. Don't stay in a depressed state or in denial. If you need help, by all means get help. It's OK to see a minister or call a psychologist.

A preacher friend was in a state of deep depression for many months. He had a wonderful family, a career in ministry and he was doing well financially. But he was in a constant state of depression for a long period of time. Finally he went to a doctor who ran some medical tests and determined that he had a chemical imbalance. The doctor prescribed medication which corrected the problem. Within days, he was past the depression and back to his old self, enjoying life once again. A chemical imbalance can be corrected with medication.

My brother-in-law also went through a dark time in his life with a severe bout of depression. It was so consuming that it almost destroyed his life. His wife found him in a basement hanging from the ceiling barely alive. She got him down and called an ambulance to take him to the hospital.

Fight The Good Fight

It took longer for him, but the doctors were able to find a medication to help him get past the depression.

Small but Brave

I coached a teenager named Tony Wolfe in a church basketball league. He was small but was a real competitor and the best player on our team. I was a terrible basketball coach that led our team to a last-place finish. That was the end of my basketball-coaching career. I always was better with the pads than the nets.

Even when Tony was grown, he was small but brave. One day, he was filling his motorcycle with gas at a local service station when three bullies approached him and tried to push him around. Tony simply took the gas hose and sprayed it on the three who were threatening him. Then he reached into his pocket and pulled out a cigarette lighter and asked if they wanted to continue the argument. They wisely declined to escalate the confrontation.

While Tony was a teenager, he went through a terrible time. His brother David told me Tony started messing around with dope and he was having a hard time quitting. The drugs depressed and altered his personality so much he placed a pistol in his mouth, pulled the trigger and tried to take his life. He was rushed to the hospital and was near death in intensive care. When I heard what he had done, I hurried to the hospital and tried to comfort his mother and father who were dear friends of mine. Miraculously, Tony survived, but he was blind. During the next 10 years, life was a real struggle for him. His parents came home one evening and found him lying at the bottom of a stairway that led to the second story near his bedroom. Evidently, he had fallen to his death. Tony's life was very tough after he had shot himself. Because of the injuries he suffered and the blindness, he wasn't able take care of himself. Those last years of his life were much, much more difficult than the torture he had faced as a teenager.

Fight The Good Fight

People start using drugs recreationally thinking they are harmless and that they can control the usage of them. I've known several people who were drug users for 20 years or more. They felt they weren't addicted to drugs and they were in control of their lives. Even though I was a drug abuser in my youth, these drug users would consider me naïve for encouraging others never to touch drugs. With hindsight being 20-20, I can review my life and clearly see how many friends and relatives destroyed and lost their lives by what began as recreational drug use, but ended being a hangman's noose.

Having come out of the 1960s drug culture and lifestyle, I've had the opportunity to talk to many alcoholics and drug addicts. I've told them about those whom we loved that lost their lives through addiction. I encouraged them to quit their horrible habits. Unfortunately, I don't know if I've been able to help one person overcome such an addiction. Being entangled in alcohol or drugs is like being in the grip of a python snake. While under its control, you are in a constant battle and feel like your life is being squeezed out of you. If you stop fighting and relax, you lose the battle and, consequently, your life.

I was very fortunate to escape from this lifestyle without becoming addicted. Many times I've felt like I was the one person who got away while alcohol and drugs imprisoned my friends and relatives. I've often wondered why it didn't completely destroy my life like it has so many others. The only explanation I have is that I gave my life to Jesus Christ, who then rescued me from Satan's grip. I feel so blessed because very few people are able to overcome this bondage. In retrospect, my thoughts today are why play with something that might kill you? I wouldn't play Russian roulette with a loaded gun? Not now or even back then. If I had it to do it again I wouldn't play with poisonous snakes, drugs or alcohol either. Potentially, they all have the same deadly, venomous bite.

Lean on Him

There's a pop song from the 1970s with the lyrics: *"Lean on me when you're not strong. I'll be your strength, I'll help you carry on."* That stirring passage evokes powerful emotions inside of me, given my journeys in this world.

I remember when Tony Dungy, the head coach of the Indianapolis Colts' National Football League team, lost his 18-year old son to suicide in fall 2005. Those who knew Coach Dungy were saying he is a man of faith, and he will need that faith in God to pull him through this terrible time. I've never met Coach Dungy, but instantly I prayed for him and his family. A little more than a year later, Dungy's team won Super Bowl XLI. I know this will not bring back his son, but sometimes in life triumph can follow tragedy, and I believe that's the case with Coach Dungy. He made the greatest statement about being happy to represent the African-American community as the first coach of his race to win the Super Bowl. But, more importantly, he said he and Chicago Bears' Coach Lovie Smith (another fine African-American coach) got their teams there by coaching the Lord's way. What a triumphant testimony to the Lord Jesus Christ after such a tragedy in his life.

In circumstances like those that befell Coach Dungy and his family, most people do not have the inner strength to handle such loss and pain. When you are carrying a burden too heavy for you to bear, go to the Lord and ask Him to shoulder the load. He can help.

Jesus said, *"Come unto me all ye that labor and are heavy laden, and I will give you rest"* (Matthew 11:28). Jesus promises rest to those who call upon him. Claim his promises as your own. Lean on him when you're not strong. He'll *be your strength he'll help you carry on*. Here are some more verses to speak as you learn to lean on the Lord:

The Lord is my rock, and my fortress, and my deliverer. 2 Samuel 22:2
Let the weak say, I am strong. Joel 3:10
T*he Lord is my strength.*" (Psalm 118:14)

The great motivational speaker Zig Ziglar says, "The more you thank God, the more he will give you to thank him for." Say things like: "*God, I thank you for providing food for me today. Lord, I thank you for clothing today. Lord, I thank you for health today. Lord, I thank you for shelter today. Lord, I thank you for strength today. I thank you, Lord, for your abundant blessings in my life today.*"

Food, Drug and Alcohol Addictions

Some of today's street drugs are so powerful that once a person has tried them, they become addicted quickly and are unable to stop using them. Satan will not let his prisoners go.

Appetite is an amazing thing. Many of us can't control our appetites. Whether it's food, nicotine, sex, drugs or alcohol, our appetite can spiral out of control.

I managed the career of middleweight professional Donald Bowers for about a year. One day, Donald and I were discussing drug addiction, specifically cocaine. Donald said, "Once is too many and a thousand times is never enough."

He was correct. Once you taste something addictive in life, one taste will just whet your appetite for more and even a thousand tastes never will satisfy your cravings.

Donald had the discipline to train very hard as a boxer and would go to the gym every day to get in good condition. When he was in shape he could run five miles in 35 minutes easily.

Donald was a very gifted athlete and because of his hard work and the help of his great amateur coach, Rayford Collins, he won two national championships as an amateur. As a pro, he compiled an outstanding 21-3 record.

Bowers also had a great sense of humor. Before a boxing match one evening, a gentleman came up to him to tell him he was there to see him fight.

Without missing a beat, Bowers asked him, "How much did you pay for your ticket?"

"Fifty dollars," the man replied.

"Well I'm going to give you $250 worth of entertainment. Would you mind paying me the difference?" Bowers asked with a chuckle.

Fight The Good Fight

Donald Bowers brings his "Rocky" impersonation to the Philadelphia landmark made famous by actor Sylvester Stallone.

I remember booking Bowers against future world champion Sumbu Kalambay in Monte Carlo.

A few weeks later when we arrived in the South of France, a week before Bowers was to face Kalambay at a contracted weight of 160 pounds, Bowers weighed about 175. I asked him why he was beyond his weight limit, and he explained to me that when he began to eat he couldn't stop eating until

Fight The Good Fight

he had stuffed himself. Like so many of us, he was addicted to food.

My youngest brother Jerry overdosed on freebase cocaine as a young man. He nearly died, and that experience scared him so much that he gave up drugs completely. However, he replaced his drug cravings with food, and has battled food addiction instead of drug addiction for nearly 20 years.

Bowers and I flew all night from New York to Nice, France, for the Kalambay fight. I sat next to Gil Clancy, the famous boxing manager and trainer. He told a story about former world middleweight champion Rodrigo Valdez, whom Clancy had managed. He said that while Valdez was in Italy waiting to defend his world championship he needed some money. He went to see the Italian boxing promoter, Rodolfo Sabatini, and asked him for an advance on his purse. Sabatini became concerned because he felt Valdez was going to hit him up for a large advance of thousands of dollars and wisely he didn't want to pay the fighter before the bout.

Sabatini asked Valdez, "How much do you need?"

To which the champion replied, "Twenty dollars."

When we arrived in Nice, France, we were transported to San Remo, Italy, where we were staying for a week before the fight. Donald had incredible discipline in many areas of his life, but he had difficulty controlling his appetite. Because of Bowers' food addiction, he couldn't control what he ate and he was beyond his contracted weight.

I was Bowers' manager, not his trainer. I didn't train him for the bout. He trained in his hometown of Jackson, Tennessee, which was 150 miles from my gym. We met at the airport before the departure and he said that his weight was fine. Normally when you train a fighter, you check their weight in the gym every day and make sure they are close to making weight before you depart for a bout.

Donald ate mostly fruit the week leading up to the fight. He made his weight for the bout, but he was very weak and he lost a unanimous decision to Kalumbay, who soon became the middleweight world champion.

Even though Donald never fulfilled his athletic potential, he has found the right path. He is now retired and is helping his old trainer, Rayford Collins, work with the kids at the Jackson Boxing Club.

Fight The Good Fight

'She's Out of Control'

Many people have food addictions that are so strong they can't control what they eat. Eating controls them. It's a sad dilemma with deep-rooted emotional issues from childhood that complicate the addiction. Compulsive eating is such a problem today that a high percentage of Americans are over-weight. Thousands of people are morbidly obese. I person-ally know of three people who were in excess of 100 pounds beyond their ideal weight and couldn't control their appetites and with their health failing all of them recently had surgery to have their stomachs stapled or banded.

Keith McKnight and I were in Detroit, Michigan, while Keith was working under the tutelage of Luther Burgess, the late, great boxing trainer. The three of us were riding in the car when we all noticed a morbidly obese woman sitting at the bus stop. Luther simply said, "She's out of control."

Slaves of the Sugar Plantation

In August 2001, boxers Warren Williams, Jake Thomas, Robert Crutcher and I traveled to the Dominican Republic, on the Island of Hispaniola in the Caribbean Sea located between Cuba and Puerto Rico, on a short-term sports mission trip with SCORE International. SCORE International is a sports mission ministry started in 1985 by Ron Bishop. He was the former head basketball coach at Tennessee Temple University in Chattanooga, before resigning to pursue sports ministry. The purpose of the organization is to evangelize through sporting events and community service.

While there, we visited the local boxing gyms, baseball parks and recreation centers. Our boxers would visit local boxing gyms and spar the local boxers. Afterward we would share the gospel with the young men. We also traveled with other college-age basketball and volleyball teams, also under the direction of Score International. These sports teams would play Dominican Republic all-star teams, and utilize this as a platform to preach the Gospel of Jesus Christ to the locals.

The Dominican people love sports, especially baseball. Baseball is a national passion in the Dominican Republic. If you ask any Dominican what he is proudest of, he will recite to you a list of great ball players.

While there, we visited the capital of Santo Domingo and spent several days in San Pedro, the hometown of baseball great Sammy Sosa. The country is a special place where nature remains unspoiled. There is about a thousand miles of coastline with white sandy beaches and the water is a beautiful shade of turquoise.

Upon our arrival on the first day and shortly before dark, Warren and I decided to wade into the beautiful sea, unaware of what awaited us. We were waist deep when the 6-foot-1, 240 pound Williams started screaming that he was under attack. I saw the sudden look of terror in his eyes and was fearful of what had victimized him. I hurriedly started in his direction and soon felt the tremendous pain that he had experienced just moments earlier. We both had stepped on sea urchins about the size of softballs and felt the burning stings as a multitude of their spines penetrated the souls of our feet. Ouch! It was so painful. For the rest of the trip we erroneously tried to remove the sea urchin spines from underneath our skin with tweezers. We learned the hard way that this is the wrong thing to do since the spine is living matter and breaks off as soon as you attempt to remove it this way. Evidently, melted wax poured onto the surface of the skin is the best way to remove them.

The Dominican people were very receptive, and after a ball game or a sparring session, they all would sit on the basketball court or on a baseball field and listen attentively to our message of hope. One native who resided in New York City but was vacationing in his homeland came to me after I had spoken to a few of his countrymen. "Sir, I want to thank you for coming to my country and telling my people about Jesus Christ," he said.

Haiti is located on the western one-third of the Island of Hispaniola and a tremendous number of Haitians sneak across the border to work in the sugar cane fields. Even though they resemble some Dominicans their dialect is much different since the Dominican Republic was a Spanish colony while Haiti was a French colony. The Dominicans try to prevent the Haitians from integrating with their countrymen and once they enter the Dominican Republic they aren't allowed to return to Haiti. Many times the Haitian government will no longer allow them back. They are in essence a people without a country.

One day while we were there our Missionary hosts took all of the sports teams to a sugar cane village. These are miserable labor camps where there are many human rights abuses.

Fight The Good Fight

To survive the Haitians have to work in the sugar cane fields. They are forced to live in these sugar cane villages where they are housed in tattered shacks. They only earn about $2 to $3 per week.

The conditions there were abysmal. There was no running water and no indoor plumbing. The Haitians live in abject poverty and are basically slaves. I noticed a company store owned by the sugar plantation in the village; it was stocked nearly completely with hard liquor. "What heartless blood suckers," I thought to myself. It was bad enough for the plantation owners to pay slave wages to these poor people, but they were getting most of the money back by selling the poor Haitians booze with which to drown their sorrows with.

I saw a beautiful little girl about 7 years old in the village. She was scared and shy, clinging to her mother's leg. One of the basketball coaches told me that he had visited the village two years before and the mother of the little girl had begged him to take her daughter to the United States with him where she could have a better life. The coach told me that he wanted to take the little girl back to the United States, but when her mother asked him to take the little girl, she began to cry hysterically and latched on to her mother tightly.

There is so much sadness and inhumanity in this present world in which we live. Often I wish I could do more to help those less fortunate than I. It's my desire to convey the word of God to offer hope to those who are living in hopelessness.

'I Have Fought the Good Fight'

Before his death, the Apostle Paul wrote his last letter to Timothy known as 2 Timothy in the New Testament, scholars set the date of the epistle around A.D. 64.

In this correspondence, Paul says to Timothy and to those of us who also are believers in Christ that we will all be judged by Jesus Christ in the presence of God. He goes on to encourage him and us to preach the word of God, do the work of an evangelist and to do our duty in ministry. He told Timothy that the time of his departure was near. Then he said, *"I have fought the good fight. I have finished the race. I have kept the faith. (2 Timothy 4: 7-8).*

Wow! What an incredible testimony for one who had been the chief of sinners before his conversion to Christ. Once he gave his life to Christ he never turned back but spent every waking hour the rest of his life telling people about salvation in Jesus Christ.

The Apostle Paul may have been the greatest Christian who ever lived. Before he became a follower of Christ, he was a murderer. He worked much like a modern day bounty hunter searching and seeking those who were believers in Jesus Christ attempting to exterminate the church. He made murderous threats against the church and persecuted and imprisoned men and women for their faith in Christ.

While on the road to Damascus on a mission to hunt down Christians and take them prisoner he was confronted by the living Jesus Christ. During his journey of more than 100 miles, he was nearing Damascus when suddenly and without warning Jesus knocked him to the ground with a flashing light from heaven. It was literally a bolt from heaven that honed in on him like a laser and knocked him down. He was blinded by the light and wasn't able to see for several days. While on the ground he heard a voice ask him, "Saul, Saul, why do you persecute me? (Acts 9: 4). When Saul, whose name later was changed to Paul, persecuted the church, he actually was persecuting Christ. Who are you Lord? Saul asked. "I am Jesus, whom you are persecuting, he replied. Now get up and go into the city, and you will be told what you must do." (Acts 9:5-6) At that moment Paul yielded his life to the savior and was converted to Christ.

God used him to preach the gospel boldly and the early church grew exponentially through Paul's ministry. For some 30 years he carried the gospel of Jesus Christ to every person who came into contact with him.

He was beaten with a whip for his faith many times, imprisoned, shipwrecked and finally executed for his belief in Christ. Church historian Eusebius who lived in the late 2nd and early 3rd centuries wrote that Paul was beheaded during the reign of the Roman Emperor Nero around 66 A.D.

Paul preached to everyone he encountered. He wasn't intimidated by anyone; he didn't show partiality to one group or another; he told everyone rich and poor how to be saved through Jesus Christ.

Today, we see churches that minister to certain classes of people but ignore the unlovely. They open their doors and welcome the beautiful people. It's easy to love the lovely. We love those who are beautiful, rich, famous, smart, athletic, clean or nice people with great personalities. Those that look like us, those who are on our socioeconomic level and speak our language are welcomed into our churches and homes.

But our Lord Jesus loved the unlovely. He loved the leper whose flesh was decaying, he loved the prostitute who had had five husbands, he loved the despised tax collectors and he loved the condemned thief being executed next to him on the cross. The Bible admonishes us in Romans 12:16 to *"Condescend to men of low estate."* Or to put it another way, we are to love the unlovely. If Christ didn't love the unlovely I would never have been saved. I was a dirty, little foul-mouthed boy who lived in a trailer park when Christ sent help to our home. There was a church with a big heart in our city that ministered to the unlovely in our community, and Christ used them to rescue our family.

I mentioned in the dedication portion of this book about my dear Christian mother living in hopelessness with a husband who drank, gambled and spent his spare time in the taverns where he often blew his paycheck and neglected the needs of his family. I'm saddened and feel somewhat guilty to tell this part of our family history but alcohol and living a wanton lifestyle has destroyed many families and would have destroyed ours but for the mercy of Christ.

So I feel that I have to share this because it might be helpful to someone else going through similar circumstances. Our family always had plenty to eat. But we didn't always have decent clothes to wear. I remember going to church during this time and the youth department was having a sock drive. Everyone there was asked to bring a new pair of socks so that they could be given to the needy in some remote part of the world. I sat there petrified that morning, hoping that no one would notice that I didn't have two socks that matched to wear. I'm sure it was difficult raising six kids on the wages my father earned at the factory. Mother was left at home with no transportation to rear a house full of children on her own. I remember how hard it was for Mother in those days and I remember how painful life was for her. I was the oldest and I saw her bitterly cry many times because of her dire circumstances. She would become so burdened that she would say, "Sometimes I wish I had never been born." But she carried on anyway.

Mother didn't have a driver's license and she didn't drive. Dad didn't go to church and he wouldn't take mother either. There wasn't a church within walking distance of where we lived. Mother didn't pray for money, a new home or things to comfort her or us. In her despair, she cried out to the Lord and asked him to send someone to take her children to church, where they might learn about Jesus and be saved. God heard and answered her prayer. As mentioned earlier, two dear saints, Stella Tuttle and Pop Sharnick, who were on bus visitation from First Assembly of God Church, knocked on our door and mother let them in. They had come to offer our family transportation to church. Mother was overwhelmed that God had answered her prayer.

As a result of that visit, during the next 15 years, our family came to Christ. Dad was saved and God prospered him financially afterward. He was abundantly helpful financially to his family, others and ministries after becoming a Christian. He and Mother went to church faithfully together for more than 30 years before he passed away in October 2006.

Printed in the United States
79316LV00001B/1-117